RUSSELL E. SMITH, JR.
1152 Bennaville
Birmingham, Mich. 48009

T3-BEA-541

GOD'S IMAGE
AND MAN'S IMAGINATION

God's Image and Man's Imagination

BY

ERDMAN HARRIS

CHARLES SCRIBNER'S SONS

NEW YORK

UNITY SCHOOL LIBRARY
DISCARD
Unity Village
Lee's Summit, Missouri 64063

Copyright © Erdman Harris 1959

This book published simultaneously in the
United States of America and in Canada—
Copyright under the Berne Convention

All rights reserved. No part of this book
may be reproduced in any form without the
permission of Charles Scribner's Sons.

A–9.59 [V]

PRINTED IN THE UNITED STATES OF AMERICA

Library of Congress Catalog Card Number 59-11438

ACKNOWLEDGMENTS

The author would like to express his gratitude to the following publishers and individuals for granting him permission to use material from their publications:

Association Press for the excerpt from *Christianity and Our World* by John C. Bennett.

Charles Scribner's Sons for material from *God at Work* by William Adams Brown.

George Allen and Unwin, Ltd., for material from "A Free Man's Worship" which appeared in Bertrand Russell, *Selected Papers.*

Harcourt, Brace and Company, Inc., for material from *The Modern Temper* by Joseph Wood Krutch, copyright, 1929, by Harcourt, Brace and Company, Inc., renewed, 1956, by Joseph Wood Krutch. Reprinted by permission of the publishers.

Harper & Brothers for material from *Our Town* by Thornton Wilder.

Harvard University Press for material from Archibald T. Davison, *Church Music, Illusion and Reality.*

BT
102
H24g

Little, Brown & Company for material from *My Idea of God* by Joseph Fort Newton.

The Macmillan Company for the selection from Sara Teasdale's *Collected Poems,* copyright by Sara Teasdale Felsinger and used with the permission of The Macmillan Company.

Random House, Inc., for material from *Inherit the Wind* by Jerome Lawrence and Robert Lee.

Union Seminary Quarterly Review and Dr. Samuel Terrien for material from his article "The Anthropology of God" in the November 1957 issue, copyrighted 1957 by Union Theological Seminary, New York.

Virginia Rice for two grace speeches from *You Can't Take It With You,* copyright © 1937 by Moss Hart and George S. Kaufman. Reprinted by permission of Virginia Rice, Agent.

FOR HARRIETTE

Contents

Preface

WITH the current increase in concern and conversation about religion, the Deity is being characterized in many ways: conventional, unconventional, and downright weird. He is the aviator's Co-pilot, the business man's Partner, the athlete's last-lap Stamina. One recent song maintains that he is a Busy Man. An evangelist speaks of him as a Porter carrying our bags when they become too heavy for us. An actress refers to him as a "Livin' Doll." He is the "Someone Up There," the "Man Upstairs," the "Fellow Upstairs." One can talk to him on the celestial telephone.

As counterpoint to this cheerfully anthropomorphic motif, we have those who share the view of a poet who was so convinced that life is "a long fool's errand to the grave" that he referred to the Power behind everything as "whatever brute and blackguard made the world."

Images of God which stimulate the imagination—that is what this book is about. My concern is that we subject all concepts to the cross-examination of intelligence, that we think about the implications of symbols often carelessly used, that we examine the consequences of taking them seriously. If Socrates can say that the unexamined life is not worth living, maybe we can agree that an unexamined faith is not worth having, even while recognizing that man cannot find faith through reasoning alone. After all, the Bible charges, "Thou shalt love the Lord thy God with all thy heart, and with all thy soul, and with all thy strength, and with *all thy mind.*"

E. H.

"Men have formed images of the mysterious Being whom they thought they found in the universe. There has been a struggle for existence and a survival of the fittest among images of Deity—a struggle still on wherever the image of Christ as the symbol of the Highest is pitted with some other image."

HENRY SLOANE COFFIN

CHAPTER 1

Images of God

"What we think of the nature of ultimate reality will determine the kind of people we are and the kind of lives we lead," a friend of mine wrote over thirty years ago. "It is true," he continued, "that for some people the kind of life they want to live determines the kind of God they choose to believe in. But, beyond a doubt, what a person thinks God to be will have a profound influence on his life."

If God is thought of as the Ultimate Power behind everything—the Fundamental Reality on which everything else depends—then it is possible to argue that everyone believes in God. Everyone acknowledges that something is basic: something was here before we arrived, it will be here after we leave—or, at least, after we graduate from this stage of existence—and it sets the limits to what it is possible for us to accomplish. The big problem, therefore, is not so much whether there *is* an Ultimate Power, but what is the *essential nature* of that Power? What conception of that Power is the most reasonable and helpful? What image of God commands the allegiance of our mind? Is the task hopeless, or does our imagination supply any clues? If we adopt a certain image of God and commit ourselves in loyalty to that image, can we feel that we are thinking along the right lines? What kind of behavior results from our belief? What habitual state of mind does our belief seem to nurture?

It is all very well for Voltaire to maintain, "If God did not exist, it would be necessary to invent Him," but if we really believed that our image of God were nothing but an invention, a pure figment of the imagination, not even a helpful clue as to the proper line to pursue to reach the truth, our faith would be empty and meaningless. If we become convinced that Ultimate Reality is impersonal rather than personal, some image of it may still be necessary, but it will be an image of something like an unconscious power, not like a conscious being. If we become convinced that Ultimate Reality is in some very real sense personal, our image will have the attributes of personality and self-awareness.

In explaining the faith that God is personal, John C. Bennett writes: "God is unique. One cannot describe God by comparing him with anything else of the same kind. The most that we can do is to find suggestions and symbols in the world of our experience . . . which seem fruitful in our thought about God. . . . To say that God is personal is to say that God is more like a person than like a thing, more like a person than like a mathematical proposition, more like a person than like a tree. . . . When we use the word 'personal' as a description of God, we mean to include only a few of the characteristics of persons: *awareness, intelligence, purposiveness, the capacity to appreciate, the capacity to respond to persons.*" * [1]

In the next chapter, we will be examining the conten-

* As almost all the footnotes supply sources for quoted material, they have been placed at the back of the book.

tion of Bertrand Russell and those who share his views that the Power behind the universe is completely impersonal. Popular thinking labels those who believe this *atheists*. We will see how careful we should be about terms of this sort. Lord Russell himself prefers the term *agnostic* to describe his position, but he does not resent the word *atheist*. In Greek the "a" before the "theos" signifies negation, and certainly it is quite fair to point out that Russell denies belief in the "theos" of the Jewish-Christian tradition; but he is too good a philosopher to be intolerantly dogmatic about his position. For instance, he once wrote, "The only thing I should ever, in my inmost thoughts, claim for any view of mine, would be that it is in a direction along which one can reach truth—never that it is truth." [2] But theists feel that, in this matter, the British philosopher's thinking is headed in the wrong direction, namely, towards unconscious power rather than personal being. It is one of the purposes of this book to clarify this problem.

But even when there is agreement about God's being in some sense personal, not much common ground has yet been established. Images differ as widely as that of "The Man Upstairs" and the "Cosmic Mathematician." A well-known movie-actress calls God a "Livin' Doll." It is true that, in certain circles, the word "doll" is a term of great appreciation. For a teen-ager to call an older person a "doll" is to pay him or her a striking compliment. Furthermore, "livin'" as an adjective means more than "living" or "lively"; it means "superlative." Therefore, God conceived as a "Livin' Doll" would be recognized as the most sympathetic unseen spiritual companion one could possibly have; but the expression will still seem presumptuously familiar to those for whom the Deity is an awesome Power to be approached with the utmost reverence and humility.

"The Man Upstairs" appears to be in the same category as the "Livin' Doll" image, as is the even more informal "the Fellow Upstairs" used by the boxer, Floyd Patterson. All this business of "up there" ("Somebody Up There Likes Me") is certainly setting our view of cosmology back several hundred years. An American runner, having just won an Olympic event, said: "When I crossed the line, I just looked up in the sky and said, 'Thanks.'" However, most of those who use expressions of this sort would, upon second thought, realize that they are employing figures of speech with no spatial significance.

There are profounder religious implications in the practice of a parent who encourages his children to pray to "Baby Jesus." ("Baby Jesus, please help Daddy, because without you he can't do anything.") The father explains that the children feel so much "closer to someone their own size." One wonders what will happen when they grow up.

This process of making the Divine very human and finite and familiar has one serious consequence that is often overlooked. The "Livin' Doll" or the "Man Upstairs," or the "Someone" or even the "He" of the song by that title, tends to be thought of as merely a friend and not, in any real sense, a judge.

> "Though it makes Him sad to see the way we live
> He'll always say, 'I forgive.'"

This is how the song "He" ends. There is no hint here of any spiritual conditions to be fulfilled, or that forgiveness costs God anything. This way of thinking is very much in line with the spirit of the proverb, "To know all is to forgive all." This may be so, but it is not what the Bible teaches. According to the Scriptures, the confrontation of the soul by God involves judgment as well as mercy.

The God of popular song and sentiment is also one who makes no serious demands on his children as to what they do with their lives. They are supposed to obey the Ten Commandments, somewhat liberally interpreted; they are not challenged to examine whether the way they make their living is God's will. A singer, thought by most people to have gained his popularity partly by the use of suggestive bodily movements, closed a television appearance recently with the words, "God has been good to me." This, of course, may have been the casual use of an unexamined phrase more akin to the friendly "gesundheit" or "God bless you," to a sneezer than a serious acknowledgement of gratitude. But the singer has been skyrocketed into prominence, not to say notoriety, by the employment of certain mannerisms which, in their effect on adolescent girls, can hardly have been approved by the Deity worshipped in our churches. Money and fame have come from the use of appeals which the normal onlooker would not connect with religion. God, actually, may not have had much to do with this young man's spectacular rise. It is very easy to do an injustice at this point, but it is still true that all sorts of people engaged in activities commonly thought to be questionable are now heard to refer to God as being "good to them," implying that he aids and abets them in what they do. The Nigerian boy who won thousands of dollars on a quiz program by rattling off answers to questions on the Bible was later discovered to have pulled the wool over the program-director's eyes: he was not a "student," as he claimed; he wanted reconciliation with his ex-wife, who was requesting $30 a week from him; however, this reconciliation might take some time because he now had another wife. When it all came out, he retired from the contest saying, "I am so embarrassed I can't concentrate on what I'm doing." Nevertheless, he stoutly maintained, "God has been good to me. He has given me a chance to win $64,000."

I once knew a worldly agnostic who, when he was dealt a good bridge hand, would mutter: "There is a God," and, when dealt a poor hand, "There is no God." This is in line with the flippant expressions heard on the golf course and elsewhere about the presence or lack of divine help, and has nothing to do with serious religion. On the other hand, I once read about the winner of the Irish sweepstakes dropping on his knees before the radio over which his good fortune was announced, and thanking God for it. Christians characteristically thank God for any good fortune that comes their way, but the implication here is that God made the horse-race come out the way it did for the benefit of the winner.

John Day, in his now famous article in *The New Yorker* magazine of July 27, 1957, entitled "The Lord Did the Rest," tells of an Olympic winner who made a second "final" spurt in the 800 metre race and passed his most serious rival at the last moment. The way he explained it was this: "I ran out of steam thirty yards from the tape and the Lord really helped me the rest of the way." It is quite possible that the Lord did, but the implications of the runner's statement are not easy to accept without critical examination. More difficult is the case of Floyd Patterson, the world's ex-heavyweight champion, who summed up the situation after one of his bouts in these words: "The Lord was in my corner. I just couldn't miss. . . . He is the one who put the heavyweight crown on my head—sure couldn't have done it without Him. . . I knew I was destined to have my hand raised from above. . . . The target was in sight and I just let fly with a short left. I could see his (the opponent's) eyes go glassy as he fell back, and I knew that if he got up it wouldn't do him any good. I just hit him, and the Lord did the rest." It may come as a shock to some that the Lord cooperates with a fighter who makes his opponent's "eyes go glassy," but this is surely no worse than God's aiding a warrior against his enemies—and history is full of struggles interpreted in that manner.

A recent headline ran, "Sooner Guard Says Prayer, Smacks Abusive Foe Harder," but the small print was less sensational. The story was about a University of Oklahoma guard who told what he does when an opposing player uses foul language on the football field: "I smile," he said, "say a little prayer for the guy and hit him harder." But, he added, "I never try to hurt an opponent, and I never have any trouble holding my Christian composure. But words like that don't make a football player better, or accomplish anything." The coach and his team usually pray three times at every game: before the opening whistle, at the half, and at the end. They never pray for victory, but that both teams will play their best. This seems several notches above the attitude of some praying athletes.

And then we have the pitcher whose special type of throw proved so difficult to hit that he won a 3-2 victory over the league-leading team, and who maintained, "I wouldn't have been able to make it work without the help of the Man Upstairs."

Students have been praying for help to pass examinations ever since examinations were invented. Most mature students do not expect God to whisper the correct answers to them, especially if they have not studied thoroughly; but prayer often steadies the nerves before a test and makes it possible for a pupil to do his best. In North India, once, a boy in a Christian missionary school showed an exceedingly broad and humane attitude towards education when he prayed: "O God, help me to pass my examination. May the whole class pass. May the school pass. May the whole world pass." The God who would answer this prayer, with no conditions attached, would surely not be the God of the Bible.

One summer day in 1957, four thousand meetings of postal employees were held, under the auspices of a benevolent association, to pray for divine aid in securing an increase in wages. The meeting in New York was led by a minister who prayed, "Bless the President of the United States. May he in his wisdom be so directed by Thy will that he may accede to these requests for an increase in postal pay." But if every group which wants more money prays for it, or prays that the President be influenced not to veto the requests, and the Secretary of the Treasury prays that the budget may be balanced, the Lord is going to have a problem.

These are but random samplings to show the nature of the situation in which God is thought of as a kind, uncritical, unseen companion who aids and abets his friends to do what appeals to the public in entertainment and sport, who is considered amenable to suggestions about pay-raises, and who demands very little from his followers except to be treated as a pal.

In the third chapter of this book we shall be examining the development of the idea of God in the Bible, and recalling how varied are the anthropomorphic images employed by the writers to make clear to the children of Israel the solicitude of the Deity for their welfare and salvation.

As Dr. Terrien of Union Theological Seminary puts it: "In the Bible, God suffers and he repents, he is angry and he hates, he is jealous, because he loves fully, he loves completely, he loves tragically. He writes, he mocks, he laughs, he swears, he cries, he shouts, he whistles, he calls like a keeper of bees, he musters his armies, he raises his banner, he brandishes his sword, he makes bare his arm. . . . He is creator not only as the utterer of the creative word but also as a potter, a gardener, a builder, a mason, a carpenter. He is a husband, a father, a mother, a hero, champion, a he-man, a warrior, one treading at the wine-press, a she-bear, a roaring lion, a soaring eagle." [3] We shall try to show how and why poetic images like these were developed in the course of Hebrew history, and how the process culminated in the conception of God as Father. We shall then, in subsequent chapters, try to explain how the image of God as Triune was conceived, how God's purposes for the world were variously interpreted by saints and seers, reformers and missionaries, and how the will of God in moral matters was and is understood by many conscientious souls, who, however, differ radically from each other. We shall try to make clear the picture of the ultimate set forth by the Mormons, the Seventh-Day Adventists, the Witnesses, the Theosophists, the Spiritualists, the Christian Scientists. We shall study the images of God we find in the hymns of our Church and the songs of our people. We shall take a glance at some of the theologies found in a sampling of the dramas of our tradition. Our purpose will be to show how varied are the images of the Divine which men of faith hold and live by, and to suggest that, where these images need correction and purification, the most helpful criterion or touchstone to use is the Bible image of One who revealed himself in his Son, and thus reconciled the world to himself.

Sometimes an image may also need the correction of science or common sense. Sometimes an image may strike us as true as far as it goes. It is important for us to examine the uses made of the various conceptions of the Divine *to see what their implications are.*

Far too often the Deity is invoked in formulae which have become nothing more than thoughtlessly used clichés, like the "Thank God" with which so many people interlard their conversation, or the "Go with God" heard so frequently in Latin countries. People also have a way of shifting gears from a practical to a pious mood and back again with such habitual facility that no incongruity is felt; yet what they say in their pious mood bears little observable relation to what they do in their practical mood. Occasionally this gear-shifting may involve deliberate hypocrisy, and there is more than a dash of hypocrisy in everyone's makeup. But more often it is an unconscious matter. Men mouth some platitude about sacrifice and straightway splurge on something as expensive as it is unnecessary. Men pray on Sunday as if they loved their neighbors and then bite an underling's head off on Monday morning at the office. Men sing sincerely in church of purity and discipline and later give way to lust and intemperance. Men sincerely affirm that God is the Father of all, and that human beings are essentially brothers, and a few days later they are indulging in some subtle form of discrimination against another human being because of his color, race or creed. The only cure for this is, as Keble's hymn puts it, "to live more nearly as we pray," to take the image of God in which we believe seriously, to think hard about what is involved in trying to serve a God who *is* love. Our image of God may be holy and challenging, but we are forever resisting his holiness and evading his challenge.

But at the moment, let us consider those cases in which the images themselves leave something to be desired, either because they seem to be based on a somewhat debatable premise, or else because they are derived by faulty reasoning from an acceptable premise. Of course, one must always recognize that most images are used analogically, symbolically, poetically, and are not meant to be taken with either scientific or prosaic literalism. But I once heard God referred to as the Great Healer by the priestess for The League for the Larger Life, who then proceeded to proclaim her faith that, if any true believer had his arm cut off in an accident, he could surely receive another one from the Lord as the result of prayer. Without attempting to limit the power of God as Healer, one has a right to wonder whether the cause of religion is served by this kind of preachment. This is more than the hyperbole so often found in the New Testament. This is an encouragement to think of the Deity as a wonder-worker, and when the hoped-for miracle does not occur, disappointment breeds disillusionment. We are often told that God can do anything ("with God all things are possible"), and that it is his divine self-restraint which prevents his intervention to produce marvels and prodigies. But reasonable faith is not promoted by wild speculation as to what God could do but does not. The image conjured up by this train of thought is of a God who anthropomorphically debates with himself, "Shall I intervene or not?" every time lightning strikes or a ship sinks or an epidemic devastates or a bomb drops or a good man is stricken by an "incurable" disease. The problem of divine self-discipline must be approached on a wider front with deeper theological insights and sharper philosophic formulations.

After one of the Navy's satellite-launching rockets was

destroyed by a technician because it began to veer from its proper course, thereby endangering the lives of those in nearby Florida communities, the man who made the decision said: "You often have only between one second and ten seconds to make up your mind, and nobody can stop me from destroying a missile except," and he paused, "maybe the Fellow up there." It was an evidence of proper humility for the naval officer to add that last phrase, but not particularly enlightening from the theological point of view.

The hecklers in Hyde Park, London, are forever challenging the supernaturalistic anthropomorphisms of the religious orators by questions such as: "If a pregnant woman were going to the hospital in a bus, would God change the traffic lights from red to green?" If the answer to this is "Yes, he surely could, and might," the query immediately arises, "What did he have against all the women who didn't make it on time?"

A friend of mine once missed a boat through a combination of circumstances over which he had no control. The boat sank with an appalling loss of life. He always believed that God had "spared" him by preventing his sailing on that particular ship. Many of us who heard him testify thus wondered what God had against the people who were drowned.

We are faced here with a great mystery, one that cannot be solved by the conception of a man-like God who "dooms" some and "spares" others for reasons best known to himself. Necessity may be the mother of invention, but disaster is the mother of improvement. We cannot expect God to save us from the consequences of our own mistakes in the realm of matter and energy. Progress in the mastery of nature comes when men learn to use her regularities for the achievement of desired ends. And just as we *use but do not break* natural laws to accomplish our purposes, so it is proper to think of God as working freely *within* his scheme of things to accomplish his purposes; the great risk he took was when he made it possible for men to achieve a measure of freedom to obey or to disobey. And yet it is this very freedom which enables men to be men, to aspire to be more, and to stumble and be less. This is not a world conducive to the happiness of whimperers or the contentment of the cowardly. God simply cannot be conceived reasonably as a cosmic nurse-maid or the purveyor of special favors or an indulgent uncle.

Buel Trowbridge recently gave a group of young people an example of the basic beneficence of the natural conditions God has laid down for our personal lives, the dependability of nature being thought of as a reflection of his reliability. Suppose, Trowbridge suggested, that we could not completely depend on the regularity of the laws of gravity or optics or metabolism or chemistry when we wished to play tennis. We throw a ball up to serve and it keeps on going out of sight like a balloon; we start to hit a forehand drive and the ball suddenly turns into gas and goes right through the racquet; we watch a return coming towards us, but a change in the law of optics causes us to see the ball five feet to the left of where it actually is; we walk out on the court to begin the game one day and melt; or we run back for a lob and explode! And yet so many preachers and pamphleteers try to make us feel that the scientist's conception of the dependability of nature is antagonistic to true religion. But if persons can use nature, the Ultimate Power behind nature can also achieve his purposes through nature. The difficulty comes when nature is conceived as a *closed* system of inevitabilities, and God as somehow *outside* the system under the necessity of intervening or interrupting the workings of that system to accomplish his ends. This image of God does not seem helpful today, nor does the image of a closed system of materialistic determinism seem helpful to the twentieth-century scientist. Such conceptions create problems for thought and faith which are insoluble in modern terms.

A misunderstanding of modern science may cause one to accept either an impersonal or a deistic view of God. If he succumbs to the former, he "accepts" the universe without inquiring into its ultimate origin or purpose. If he settles for the latter, he imagines that God created the universe, established its laws, and then sat back as an interested but aloof spectator, giving man a measure of freedom within the framework of immutable law, and watching to see how the human drama eventually will work out. If this were true, the divine help that anyone would receive would come simply from his fulfilling natural conditions which were established at creation. This concept can be expressed in the saying, "God helps those who help themselves," and there is so much truth in this that some think of it as the complete story. We can, however, understand what Sir Wilfred Grenfell meant when he said, "God himself cannot save the world without us. This is for me a sufficient explanation of why we are here." I imagine everyone knows the story of the parson who stopped beside a field of corn as "high as an elephant's eye" and said to the proud farmer, "Don't forget that you could not have raised this crop without God," to which the farmer replied, "You ought to have seen it two years ago when God was working alone." Over the archway of a French medical school is the carved inscription, "I dressed his wounds, God healed him"; this is the true attitude of the humble theist, but the deist is inclined to believe that God only heals when laws established billions of years ago are fulfilled, and the healing therefore takes place automatically and, in a sense, impersonally. Theology must help people to wrestle with problems of this type so that they will not feel restricted in their choice of intellectually respectable positions to naturalism or deism.

There are many people who give up the intellectual struggle by adopting an agnostic attitude about much of "God's activity." They have a suspicion there are things which God does directly, and other things which he does indirectly through agencies which he has set in motion but which he does not manage in detail. William Cowper, the English poet, once decided to throw himself into the Thames on a densely foggy night in London. He found a cab and urged the driver to seek the Embankment. After being hopelessly lost in the fog for a considerable time, he got impatient, leaped out of the cab, only to find himself home again. It is reported that he gave up the idea of suicide, went to his room and wrote the hymn,

> "God moves in a mysterious way
> His wonders to perform."

It would be a bold man who would deny that God may not have had a hand in saving William Cowper that night, but it would be a bolder man who would argue that God personally guided the horse! To achieve a satisfying and reasonable faith, it is important to examine with great care the implications of the statements about God we make and the ideas about God we entertain. It will not do to pray Beerbohm Tree's agnostic's prayer, "O God, give me the faith to believe in those things which the common sense Thou hast given me tells me are not true." Life is full of mystery.

Faith is a daily necessity. But we do not have to suspend our critical faculties when confronted by something we do not understand. As I shall try to show, we have an obligation to be skeptical about the whys and wherefores of things; it has been said that although faith is crucial for living, it is doubt that gets you an education.

A historian once remarked that the reason why Napoleon failed was that God became bored with him. Does this mean that God, who for a while was interested in the Corsican adventurer, and anxious to see what he was going to do with his human freedom, finally lost interest?

Victor Hugo, in *Les Miserables,* suggests that it was not possible for Napoleon to have won the battle of Waterloo. "Why? On account of Wellington, on account of Blücher? No! On account of God. . . . Napoleon had been denounced in the Infinite, and his downfall had been determined. He was obstructing God. Waterloo is no mere battle; it is a change of front on the part of the universe." This is, of course, merely a nineteenth-century version of the prophetic conviction, voiced over and over again in the Bible, that the affairs of men are in the hands of God, and that a cruel and unjust conqueror will eventually fail. But what has to be assumed here to believe this? Does it mean that the universe which God has created is so constructed that evil will always turn out to be self-defeating, that there will always be freedom-loving fighters against tyranny who will bring it to naught? Or does it mean that God, as an active personal agent, consummates the downfall of tyranny in a way which would never happen if nothing but the normal forces in our world were allowed to work? Granted that we face a mystery here, I maintain that there are more reasonable and less reasonable ways of thinking about the matter, and that some preachers, for instance, who use pious generalizations do their congregations a disservice which is not at all either desirable or necessary.

Einstein once devised a motto which may be found over a fireplace in Princeton: "God is a scientist, not a magician." Sir James Jeans speaks of God as the Great Mathematician. Einstein wrote: "The most beautiful and most profound emotion we can experience is the sensation of the mystical. . . . He to whom this emotion is a stranger, who can no longer wonder and stand wrapt in awe, is as good as dead. To know that what is impenetrable to us really exists, manifesting itself as the highest wisdom and the most radiant beauty which our dull faculties can comprehend only in their most primitive forms—this knowledge, this feeling is at the center of true religiousness." [4] At another time he said, "My religion consists of a humble admiration of the illimitable superior spirit who reveals himself in the slight details we are able to perceive with our frail and feeble minds. That deeply emotional conviction of the presence of a superior reasoning power, which is revealed in the incomprehensible universe, forms my idea of God." [5]

Kepler, looking up from his mathematical computations, prayed, "I think thy thoughts after Thee, O God."

Thornton Wilder, in "Our Town," gives the address of a letter to one of the characters in the play, as

"Jane Crofut
The Crofut Farm
Grover's Corners
Sutton County
New Hampshire
United States of America
Continent of North America
Western Hemisphere

The Earth
The Solar System
The Universe
The Mind of God."

Is it helpful thus to speak of "the Mind of God"? Is God conscious, personal, super-personal? Does he care about us? Does he act, or simply look on? How does he guide us? What does he want us to do and be? Is it right for us to think of him familiarly as the "Man Upstairs"? Is he interested in our "peace of mind"? Does he get angry with us if we sin? These are some of the questions with which we shall be dealing in the pages that follow. We shall urge that any statements we make about God be firmly grounded in a reasonable understanding of what those statements mean in terms of his character and attributes. This is to be a study, not so much of the *truth* of religious concepts as of the *implications* of these concepts if their truth is accepted on faith.

In spite of the fact that many people today *say* they believe in God, even though they use that term in a variety of ways, there are still many who *do not*. One of my high-school students, brought up by parents who claim they do not believe in God, once asked me in class, "What do you think is God's attitude towards atheists?" I replied that I would first like to know their description of the God they do *not* believe in; I might find that I did not believe in him either. Then I would like to know something about the way they had been brought up, why they reacted negatively to a conception to which many extremely intelligent and thoughtful people react positively. I said that God, if he exists, would understand thoroughly why people do or do not accept certain statements about him, and would be the only one capable of assessing their moral and intellectual responsibility. This general line of thinking, when reported to the parents by the student, caused great merriment in the family, according to the report I received!

It is a fact that many thinking people are thrown off by what preachers and parishioners say about God. An unwise statement about a very much beloved member of a family who dies a painful death from a disease for which no cure has yet been discovered, may have an unfortunate effect on young people. "God took him" suggests all sort of conceptions to a sensitive and thoughtful child, most of them untrue to the God of the New Testament. A man who has been through the depths of attempted suicide resulting in permanent disability, but who nevertheless has now made a courageous adjustment, writes, "God cannot be both all good and all powerful. . . . I cannot believe in a God who is consequently either malevolent, incompetent or indifferent." There are many people today who dismiss theism with some such brief statement. I hope this book may help those who read it to see that Christian theology has never had any interest in a God who is either "malevolent, incompetent, or indifferent." Christianity would have died long ago if this were true. The problem is not adequately stated in those terms. We hope to show how the problem should be stated. It is basically a question of the *true nature* of the Ultimate Power from which all things come and on which all things depend. Stated carefully, with allowances made for the inevitable mystery of infinity when tackled by finite minds, belief in God may seem far more reasonable than its opposite. But if it is to become so, the issue must be defined so that the implications for life fit in with, and do not collide head on with, the carefully accumulated knowledge which conscientious thinkers have been building up for centuries.

CHAPTER 2

The God of the Theist

Many men believe that the carefully accumulated knowledge which conscientious thinkers have been building up for centuries makes belief in any sort of God impossible. I once knew a scientist who felt this way, and the effect of his "atheism" on his life would not encourage anyone I know to share his belief. He started out as a teacher, but soon left education for money-making. He had a suicide-pact with a friend that when life became unendurable each would help the other to end it all; this has not yet been carried out. But he insisted on a Christian funeral for his wife; when the minister protested that the words of the service would be a denial of the widower's entire philosophy, the reply was, "She would have liked it."

He always insisted that the place to find real happiness on earth is where you see a dog chasing a rabbit. If a dog ever became capable of stopping to ask, "Why should I be chasing this animal?" his happiness would be at an end. Joseph Wood Krutch, in *The Modern Temper*, written toward the end of the 1920s, says, "Nature, in her blind thirst for life, has filled every possible cranny of the rotting earth with some sort of fantastic creature, and among them man is but one—perhaps the most miserable of all, because he is the only one in whom the instinct of life falters long enough to enable it to ask the question, 'Why?'"[1]

One of the most familiar and eloquent statements of the atheistic position is to be found in Bertrand Russell's "A Free Man's Worship," first published in 1902:

"That man is the product of causes which had no prevision of the end they were achieving; that his origin, his growth, his hopes and fears, his loves and his beliefs, are but the outcome of accidental collocations of atoms; that no fire, no heroism, no intensity of thought and feeling, can preserve an individual life beyond the grave; that all the labors of the ages, all the devotion, all the inspiration, all the noonday brightness of human genius, are destined to extinction in the vast death of the solar system, and that the whole temple of man's achievement must inevitably be buried beneath the debris of a universe in ruins—all these things, if not quite beyond dispute, are yet so nearly certain, that no philosophy which rejects them can hope to stand. Only within the scaffolding of these truths, only on the firm foundation of unyielding despair, can the soul's habitation henceforth be safely built."[2]

This is a remarkable phrasing of the belief—conscious or unconscious—of many people. Note particularly the words "pre-vision" and "accidental." Lord Russell is affirming that when the world broke off from the sun, or when the tremendous explosion took place which gave birth to what we call our "system" (the modern conception of the beginning), there was *nothing* anywhere in the universe which *knew* what was going on, or what possibilities lay ahead. The "causes" which produced the universe were completely unconscious and impersonal. Furthermore, what happened was a cosmic "accident." It happened the way it did by chance. It might have happened some other way, with different results, if a different "collocation of atoms" had occurred. Therefore, there is no God, no immortality. Eventually, there will be a running-down of the clock, or another cosmic accident, and that will be that. There will be nothing left to show for anything that was ever accomplished anywhere. Even if there were ruins remaining on a cold and uninhabited earth, there would be no mind to know what they meant. The rise and fall of civilizations might just as well not have taken place. Socrates and Plato and Aristotle, Buddha and Confucius, Sophocles and Shakespeare, Bach and Beethoven, Michelangelo and Rembrandt, all will have made their indispensable contributions to the culture of which they were a part, but at long last, when the earth becomes uninhabitable, there will be no one anywhere to remember them, no Deity to recall their achievements. Jesus, a winsome and powerful human figure, will turn out to have been profoundly mistaken, and when the last of his followers dies, there will die with him the belief that the Galilean revealed the essential nature of the ultimate and conquered death itself.

Notice that the original statement contains the words "these truths, although not quite beyond dispute." The young Bertrand Russell was a good enough philosopher to realize that a dash of agnosticism was needed to temper what might otherwise have been dismissed as mere dogmatism. And yet the statement proceeds that these "truths" are "so nearly certain" that "no philosophy which rejects them can hope to stand"; and the climax comes with the somewhat florid passage, "only on the firm foundation of unyielding despair can the soul's habitation henceforth be safely built." A modern Greek writer puts it, "Only on the abyss may man build the affirmative structure of his life," and says, "I hold Death like a black banner and march on!"

Any thinking person must admit that this *may* be true, but Lord Russell cannot be certain of it, nor can we be absolutely certain of its opposite. If the atheistic view of life is correct, then a personal God is nothing but a figment of man's imagination, and any sort of life beyond the grave is merely a pious hope, or, for cruel and wicked men, an unnecessary worry.

Some of those who share this view agree with Krutch who speaks of man as "miserable." When he wrote *The Modern Temper* he did not even believe that man could make much of this world: "The victims of the modern temper do not and never expect to believe in God; but unlike their spiritual fathers, the philosophers and scientists of the 19th century, they have begun to doubt that rationality and knowledge have any promised land into which they may be led." [3]

H. L. Mencken, in the early twenties, tried to laugh off theism by saying:

"To sum up:

"1. The cosmos is a gigantic fly-wheel making 10,000 revolutions a minute.

"2. Man is a sick fly taking a dizzy ride on it.

"3. Religion is the theory that the wheel was designed and set spinning to give him the ride." [4]

Krutch, rather than laugh it off, recommends the stiff upper lip: "Ours is a lost cause and there is no place for us in the natural universe, but we are not, for all that, sorry to be human. We should rather die as men than live as animals." [5]

James Gould Cozzens feels that the universe is a "dreadful eyeless face," indifferent to and unmindful of man; but he recommends stoic endurance, and a courageous return to the fight after being knocked down. He makes Colonel Ross in *Guard of Honor* say: "If mind failed you seeing no pattern, and heart failed you seeing no point, the stout stubborn will must be up and doing. . . . A man must stand up and do the best he can with what there is."

Krutch accuses Russell, Unamuno and Santayana of arguing that the way of salvation for men lies in a sort of "ironic belief, in a determination to act as though one still believed the things which once were really true." [6] But Russell's "faith" seems to be more along the line of making the best out of *known* possibilities. For instance, after describing the better world within our reach if only we would apply the findings of science to our daily life, he says, "Such a world is *possible;* it waits only for men to wish to create it. Meantime, the world in which we exist has other aims. But it will pass away, burned up in the fire of its own hot passions; and from its ashes will spring a new and younger world, full of fresh hope, with the light of morning in its eyes." [7]

This may not sound much like basing one's philosophy on the "firm foundation of unyielding despair." Actually Lord Russell has poured out his time and talent generously in the cause of a better life for mankind. Disbelief in a personal God sometimes produces apathy or libertinism or cynicism or spiritual paralysis, but not at all necessarily. Julian Huxley, as of 1957, writes: "Civilized man is beginning to realize that he can, if he so wishes, in large measure model the world in accordance with his desires," [8] and goes on to give an inspiring picture of what our life might be like if we used the knowledge we now have in the service of humanity; Huxley rejects all personalistic theologies, but works optimistically at his scientific and philanthropic tasks.

An atheist is bound to reject the notion that there is a transcendent Power that works *through* nature. He looks upon the theist's belief in a God who sustains the natural order as erroneous and unnecessary. He feels that this is only a more sophisticated form of animism. The theist, on the other hand, sees all the difference in the world between the notion that unseen spirits, good or bad, inhabit natural objects, move them around, cause them to act, and the belief that God in his providence has established the natural order within which events take place with dependable regularity.

When a savage, using a path through the jungle which runs beneath a cliff, is nearly struck by a falling stone, it is natural for him to feel that some malevolent spirit has it in for him, and that he should avoid that path in the future. Animism is the "science" of the primitive.

Once, my wife and I were spending a sunny morning at a lake in Switzerland, which was surrounded on three sides by immense cliffs, crossed at intervals by a score of waterfalls. I thought it would be amusing to take a shower under one of these; it was ice-cold, and very refreshing. However, the moment I stepped from under it, several tons of rock crashed down on the very spot I had occupied. If I had been living in prehistoric times, or in a primitive society, I would surely have attributed that near accident to an unfriendly incorporeal being. Or, if I had been a member of any one of a number of Protestant sects, I might have felt that God had somehow warned and spared me for an important share in his work. But if I were a scientifically minded atheist or agnostic I would not attribute the threat to my life to the direct operation of a spiritual being; nor would I, probably, as a liberal Christian. I would merely recognize that when the center of gravity of a certain number of precariously balanced stones was disturbed, they fell, and it was only luck that I moved out of their path in time. This, of course, would not prevent me from being thankful, and from resolving to do better with my borrowed time.

Some friends of ours were playing golf with their daughter and the club professional one Saturday when a sudden electrical storm caught them unaware. The parents were rushing towards the clubhouse a few yards ahead of the others, when a terrific bolt of lightning struck and killed the girl, and temporarily paralyzed the professional. A scientist would make nothing philosophical out of this, except the inevitable operation of a bolt from cloud to ground when the proper conditions were fulfilled. There is no need to assume that the forces of nature selected a fine and promising girl for destruction, and deliberately spared all others who were playing that same afternoon. The foursome had no way of knowing, because of the suddenness of the storm, what danger they were in. They knew enough not to take shelter under a tree; they could not know enough to realize their vulnerability on the open fairway. Lightning is said to kill an average of one American a day, and do an average of $50,000 damage a day in this country. It is not helpful to think that these deaths and this destruction are planned by a God who has it in for particular victims or the owners of the damaged property.

Jesus said that God "makes his sun rise on the evil and on the good, and sends rain on the just and on the unjust." [9] The great elemental natural forces do not consider the moral quality of those who either benefit by or suffer from them. You cannot attribute drought in Connecticut to a lack of virtue in its citizens, or rain in the Adirondacks to the possession of superior virtue by the people of upper New York State. Jesus seems to be quite clear that *morality and meterology are not connected.* But Jesus does use the phrase, "that you may be sons of your Father who is in heaven, for he *makes* . . . and *sends.*" For an atheist the sun and the rain are merely "sent" by nature, which has fallen into certain patterns of behavior, so that when conditions are fulfilled, particular results occur; no one "sends" rain, or "makes" the sun shine on anyone. The liberal Protestant might agree that it is not reasonable to think of God as sitting behind some huge instrument-panel in a celestial weather station, and sending or withholding rain for specific reasons, but he would certainly believe that God is ultimately behind the weather, that everything that happens is in the hands of the Deity. He might feel very uncomfortable actually praying for rain, but he would not rule God out of the creation of conditions which, in fact, have been highly favorable to the development of life and mind and civilization on this planet.

In this sense, the liberal Christian thanks God for making possible all the rich and rewarding experiences of men. He believes in God as the source of all good actually realized and felt; he also believes that there is much potential good which can be, but is not now, being realized. He believes that God wants man to clear away the obstacles which prevent him from achieving a satisfying life. He believes that God permits the *possibility* of evil as an inevitable accompaniment to freedom, though he does not feel that God *wills* evil. He does not have to believe in any form of the "celestial instrument panel," manned by an anthropomorphic Deity, acting *directly* to accomplish his purposes. But he does believe in using personal terms for God, praying to God *as if* he were a person present, and attributing to him those characteristics which were taught by and revealed in Christ.

We can make this position clearer by considering, first, the views of certain scientifically oriented thinkers who, though they do not use personal terms for God, would dislike intensely to be thought "atheists." Nature, for them, is the totality of things. There is no transcendental reality "outside" of nature. When they attempt to construct an idea of God, they do as Henry N. Wieman does, and conceive of the Divine as that "Something upon which human life is most dependent for its security, welfare and increasing abundance," [10] but which is still part of nature; or as Edward S. Ames does, conceiving of God as the "personification and idealization of nature" and "society," analogous to one's conception of Alma Mater or Uncle Sam; [11] or as John H. Dietrich does, conceiving of God as "the mighty spirit of humanity." [12] Dietrich maintains that he cannot believe in a "power outside of man himself that fashions individual character and human society." Wieman believes that there is "Something" in some sense "outside of man" on which he depends, but which is not to be thought of as personal or supernatural. And these three thinkers, and those who share their views, believe that a truly religious life is possible, and have been at some pains to emphasize their belief in a valid "religious experience" for man, and even the reception of what might be called divine guidance.

There are present in the cosmos, say these men, possibilities of both good and evil, not because they were "put there" (at least, we know nothing of the ultimate "how"), but because that is the way things are. Dietrich has one passage which closely parallels the paragraph from Bertrand Russell which I quoted earlier in this chapter:

"So I believe that the whole process and development of the universe from the beginning until now has been the result, not of a personal creator and ruler outside of it, setting it in motion, directing its course, and shaping its development, but of the working of some inward motive power—a power which at first perhaps was an unconscious impulse, but which has developed into self-consciousness in humanity, the highest expression of that power on this planet, and its controlling force in so far as human affairs are concerned. Until recently this impulse no doubt pushed forward blindly, all unconscious of what its end might be; but, at last in man it has assumed the proportions of consciousness, and henceforth will be consciously directed by humanity . . . Think of it: we are shaping the destiny of a planet. We are not, as previously supposed, oppressed by having to do the will of a superior power. The only power that in any way controls us is the collective will of humanity, and of that we are the creators. We can mark out our own goal and choose our own path to that goal; and no power outside of ourselves can defeat the purpose of man." [13]

Put this way, the view is less convincing to most theists than is Bertrand Russell's stark statement ending in "despair." When Dietrich says that "no power outside of ourselves can defeat the purpose of man," it sounds suspiciously like whistling in the dark. From the human standpoint man is, as Tennessee Williams calls him, "a beast that dies," and there is certainly nothing "inside" ourselves that can change that fact. So both the atheist and the scientifically oriented religious person have to learn to live without faith in anything personally transcendent that cares, and without hope for any life beyond this.

Emerson once wrote, "We are begirt with laws which

execute themselves. They are out of time, out of space, out of circumstance; thus, in the soul of man there is a justice whose retributions are instant and entire. He who does a good deed is instantly ennobled. He who does a bad deed is by the action itself contracted."[14] Emerson calls the operation of natural law "active," but this is really only a figure of speech. It is not self-consciously active in the sense that persons are active, but rather in the sense that a stream is active when a dam breaks.

Thinkers of the type we have been discussing do not feel the need of a universe undergirded by a power purposely striving for goodness. All they ask is a universe which contains genuine possibilities for the development of the good life. They may or may not wish to call the sum-total of these tendencies "God," as the average man often calls the sum-total of other tendencies "Mother Nature." If they wish to—and believe that there is some unity to, or behind, or in, these tendencies—they can build a sort of theism which differs from ordinary theism in that God is not conceived as a conscious Being.

According to Walter M. Horton, they would argue:

(1) "God is my own better self." The promptings of my own better self—the more unselfish, socially minded self—are divine guidance for me. I receive directions as to what I should do when I relax and am anxious to know the best. But I do not consider such "guidance" as coming from Someone, or as giving evidence of the existence of a Someone.

(2) "God is all that is best in our human heritage." This forms a norm by which I can check the promptings of my own better self. Also, when I expose my mind to the great thoughts of the past, I am fulfilling the conditions for new

illumination which often comes to me as freshly *as if* it were given to me by Someone beyond myself.

(3) "God is a vast cosmic drift or trend toward harmony, fellowship, and mutual aid, whereby our efforts to create a just equilibrium in human affairs are supported and sustained." "I believe there is such a drift," says the non-personalistic thinker, "enshrined in the very structure of the universe. There are, of course, antagonistic drifts and processes, but the laws of life in general make for cooperation, and if we violate them we suffer death, division, and unhappiness. By the same token, if we obey them we enjoy life, harmony and well-being." [15]

It is, however, very difficult to imagine praying to a God conceived as one's own "best self," or as "all that is best in our human heritage," or "a vast cosmic drift or trend towards harmony, fellowship and mutual aid." This is not the God of the Bible. A worship service, based on this conception, could use the forms of traditional prayer only in a figurative, symbolic, or poetical way, completely detached from any hint that the terms used pointed in the direction of a genuine reality. Tillich says that the only non-symbolic statement that can be made about God is that "the being of God is being-itself." [16] But there is a tremendous difference between various symbolic statements. Some are anthropomorphic to a high degree: "He that sitteth in the heavens shall laugh." [17] Some are anthropomorphic only in the sense of implying that God is better thought of as personal, super-personal, or supra-personal than as impersonal, unconscious, and totally without any of those characteristics which we associate with self-conscious being: "God is a spirit: and they that worship him must worship him in spirit and in truth." [18] Most of the Lord's Prayer is phrased in symbolic language of this second type rather than of that represented by the Second Psalm. But both of these utterances have the common denominator of reference to a being who, in some sense, is conceived as higher in our personalistic scale of values than we—infinitely higher, we would affirm; whereas to pray to "Our Father" but mean by that only "all that is best in our human heritage" or some "vast cosmic drift" is to apply a personal term to something which is, no matter what else it may be, impersonal.

This kind of personification is used freely by Fourth of July orators who apostrophize "America," or "Uncle Sam." It is also found in the Psalms: "If I forget thee, O Jerusalem, let my right hand forget her cunning." [19] It is found in the Gospels, where Jesus cries, "O Jerusalem, Jerusalem. . . . how often would I have gathered thy children together, even as a hen gathereth her chickens under her wings, and ye would not!" [20] But when Jesus taught his followers to pray, "Our Father," he meant the expression to convey his faith in an unseen personal being with whom all men could have vital communion. This is quite different from a poetical apostrophe; that is not personalizing something essentially impersonal, for literary or oratorical or emotional effect; this is an affirmation of faith in the personal nature of the unseen.

It may be difficult to pray to God as "being-itself," but once we realize that such an unsymbolic assertion means the reality on which all things depend, or the power in which we live and move and have our being, we are then free to use symbolic concepts in our devotional life. Of course, God is *not* masculine, though we address him as Father. It is almost impossible to use language accurately in this connection. We obviously cannot call God "it"; or, if we do, it is an "it" *beyond* personality, *above* the imaginary top of our value scale, rather than an impersonal force *below* the other end. But even the use of "above" and "below" is figurative; as human beings we seem bound to think in human terms.

We feel that we know why Jesus used the term "Father" for God rather than others more commonly employed in the Hebrew tradition: an oriental potentate (Lord of Lords, and King of Kings) would have power over his subjects, but *not necessarily* love for them; a father (in Biblical times) would have power over his children *and*, if he were a true father, love for them. An oriental mother might have lots of love but very little power; although the Christian Science service includes a prayer beginning, "O Great Father-Mother God," and thereby tries to bring the parental concept up to date. In the early days of the Woman Suffrage movement, an ardent votes-for-women advocate is said to have told her child: "Put your trust in God, and *she* will help you." In matriarchal forms of society, the Divine is often pictured as feminine. The difficulty comes from our inability to refer to anything personal without using pronouns which are either masculine *or* feminine. And yet, if we realize this, there should be no real confusion.

The concept of a God who can, in full theological honesty, be thought of as personal—more intensely personal than anyone of whom we have earthly experience, yet free from the limitations which bodily conditions and human psychology enforce upon us—may be as wrong as the young Bertrand Russell thought it was, but at least it is definite enough to be an intelligible article of faith. The writer of the 103rd Psalm believed that "as a father pitieth his children, so the Lord pitieth them that fear him." Jesus apparently agreed; the closest analogy to God in human experience was, for him, human fatherhood at its best, raised to the nth degree. He urged us to think of "how much more" God could be expected to do than men. It was as if Jesus said, "Take the conception of the best father imaginable, endow it with infinite wisdom, power and love; and, limited though your finite minds are and must be, it can become for you an adequate, and not a misleading, symbol for the Power which is from everlasting to everlasting."

Now let us take a further and closer look at the idea of God as personal, which so many people find it difficult, if not impossible, to believe. Christian theologians do not see how one can sufficiently explain the "better self" of man, the consciousness of the good and the ideal, or the "cosmic drift towards harmony, fellowship, and mutual aid" (if there is one) without postulating the existence of an absolute being whose presence is revealed in these things. When Wieman calls God "Something," Christian theists feel that this is placing the power thought of as the ground of religious experience lower in the scale of values than the highest actually encountered in experience. When God is looked upon as a "process of integration" and that alone, this definitely limits the idea of the Divine to a *condition* for life and not an agent. The theist feels that the conception of a process, unconscious of itself, somehow built into the structure of things, is about on the same level of value as gravity, or some other impersonal force. He can believe that gravity has no "pre-vision" of the results of its action. Even though gravity is now thought of in terms of a magnetic field, it is still something unconscious of itself.

It may be that our scale of values, so obvious to us, is not the scale of values of the universe as a whole, or of its underlying power. But it is hard to get away from the conviction that a plant is higher in the scale of values than a stone. A stone is now recognized as a marvel of intricately organized energy, but it does not exhibit what we call life, whereas a plant or a flower not only contains matter, as marvellous, physically and chemically, as the matter in a stone, but it also exhibits life, the power of growth, even a limited power of self-repair. To us a geranium may be more interesting than a stone, and an intelligent and beloved household pet more interesting than a geranium. Apes have not only rudimentary minds but the ability to solve problems, which is one obvious evidence of intelligence. Kohler's apes figured out that by standing boxes on end they could reach the bananas hanging overhead in their cage.

But even the most advanced ape or chimpanzee gives no evidence of the capacity for abstract thought, literary composition, or self-awareness in the sense in which we apply that term to human beings. And when we meet and know exceptional examples of humanity, we feel that we are in the presence of something way up at the top of our scale of values. This scale does not seem to be anything we "make up." It seems natural and axiomatic. Possibly this is because we, being human, can only have the inner experience of *human* consciousness. We do not know how it "feels" to be a dog, much less a plant or a stone. We assume that a dog has feelings; we are not so sure about plants; we are rather sure that stones do not. But we are in no position to be dogmatic about this.

Some Eastern philosophies affirm that animals and insects have "souls," and that these "souls" are used over and over again, in different bodies, in a great and complex drama of reincarnation. I know of no way of proving that this whole concept is false, although I have a feeling in my bones that it is. But even Albert Schweitzer, obedient to his doctrine of "reverence for life," makes distinctions between living things: snakes, dogs, children.

Dean Inge once wrote, "The naturalist may account for nature, but not for himself as an observer of nature." When someone said, "Astronomically speaking, man is insignificant," the reply was, "Astronomically speaking, man is the astronomer." Operating on our own scale of values, we would make bold to say that an astronomer is higher in that scale than a star, which probably does not even know it is a star. After all, the astronomer is aware of himself, and knows what he is doing when he tries to measure the size, composition, and distance from the earth of a star revealed in his telescope. To a thinking human being, mere bigness is no criterion of greatness or value. A man, halfway in size between an atom and a star, seems high up on the scale because he embraces in his being not only the marvellous intricacy of matter, the mystery of life, the capacity to think, but the awareness of being a person. Jesus said that God valued persons above everything else. ("How much then is a man better than a sheep?" "Ye are of more value than many sparrows.")

The atheist may also believe that a man is "better than a sheep" or "of more value than many sparrows," but he would believe that this is merely his own or humanity's evaluation. The universe itself has no such scale of values. It takes a person to have a scale of values; since he believes there is no cosmic Person, there can be no cosmic value-scale. But the Christian theist keeps coming back to the idea that since the power behind the universe produced personality, that power must be as high on the scale of values as personality is, if not infinitely higher. He finds it incredible that Jesus should have been produced by an unconscious, blind power; it seems much more reasonable to imagine that Jesus was produced by a power rightly conceived as way beyond the top of the scale; that is, as either personal, super-personal or supra-personal. Christians believe that this Infinite and Personal Spirit revealed himself to us in history and in Christ; when theists reason about this revelation, they see no escape from the conclusion that it takes a Person to account for personality. This line of thought may leave the atheists cold; but theists find it much easier to believe than its opposite. Dr. H. E. Fosdick puts it this way: "When anybody tells me that the explanation of the soul and the kingdom of values, in which alone the soul truly lives, lies in the fortuitous arrangement of matter, that seems more incredible than the strangest religious creed." [21] The Psalmist puts it succinctly: "He that formed the eye, shall he not see?" [22]

The theist would paraphrase Lord Russell's early description of the nature of the universe, as presented to us by science, in some such way as this: That man is a product of a Power which, in some real sense, understood the possibilities of development in the universe from the very beginning, that man's hopes and fears, his loves and his beliefs are the outcome of a creative purpose which has, nevertheless, given him freedom to obey or disobey; these truths, although not completely certain, seem yet more reasonable than the contrary. The theist is thoroughly cognizant of the inevitable end of the world. Sooner or later the vast temple of man's achievement *will* inevitably be buried beneath the debris of a *physical* universe in ruins. But this has no bearing on the faith that somehow, in another dimension, it may be, souls will survive with God. These beliefs may be more enduring than those which leave no room for the Deity or immortality. Christians believe that it is only on the firm foundation of unyielding faith and hope that the soul's habitation henceforth may be safely built.

However, when one uses the category or personality to characterize the Deity, he must admit that the atheist or agnostic is at liberty to insist upon a more careful use of it than is sometimes made. To conceive of God as *a* Person may be too anthropomorphic for comfort. Personality appears to some a limiting concept; and when it is freed from human limitations, it may seem to lose all concrete significance. When Einstein talks of the "illimitable superior spirit who reveals himself in the slight details we are able to perceive with our frail and feeble minds," this may impress us as an extraordinarily tenuous and unhelpful idea of God. Einstein claimed that his conviction was "emotional," not cold or abstract; but his expression of it is vague. He believed in the "presence of a superior reasoning power revealed in the incomprehensible universe." This certainly escapes anthropomorphism, but ends in what the common man may find a very formless and watered-down conception. To Einstein, marvelling at how the universe works in dazzlingly beautiful mathematical ways, God as a Mathematician (Sir James Jean's idea), a Mind, a Reasoning Power must have seemed to him the highest compliment he could pay to the divine mystery. Dr. Fosdick puts it, "Wherever mind goes, the universe answers mind, as though mind had made it, and so mind could understand it." The atheist still would not be convinced by this assumption of an intelligence behind phenomena, the secret of which can only be understood by intelligence. The theist would recognize Einstein's statement as a minimum belief, the least one could hold and still be devoted to the primacy of mental and spiritual values; the theist would go much farther than this, and run the risk of being called an anthropomorphist.

Dr. William Adams Brown writes: "The characteristic

thing about personality as we know it in ourselves is not that it is limited—that is common to all finite and relative experience—but that it succeeds, at least in part, in transcending its limitations . . . we are not persons all the time. Only in our best moments are glimpses given to us of the larger world just across the veil . . . when we say of God that he is personality, we are not limiting God to such fleeting experiences of transcendence. Rather we are confessing our faith that what in us is potential to him is actual, and what in us is occasional in him is constant."[23] If we believe that God is in any sense personal, we must stretch the concept to infinity before it becomes adequate to meet our intellectual and spiritual needs. What it means to us to be personal and what it means to God is surely like comparing a candle to the sun, but both candle and sun give off light and heat, and therefore are akin. Our sense organs bring to us the raw stimuli of existence to be translated into order and meaning by an unbelievably complex cortical process. After that, we have to make up our minds how to react. Our reactions depend upon past experience, native equipment, semantic conditioning, emotional tone and many other factors which influence what we do and what we think about what we do. Imagine for a moment the theist's view of God's reaction to a situation: any one situation for him is just one of an infinite number of happenings which are immediately present to his consciousness, without any spacial limitations to his interest and apperception.

A number of years ago, a popular magazine carried a cartoon of a boy about to say his prayers when he suddenly sees his sister kneeling by the bed saying hers. He blurts out, "Oh! the line's busy." Theists believe that God can hear the simultaneous prayers of the more than two and a half billion denizens of this planet, and pay as much attention to each as if he were the only one praying. This may be true, but it stretches the average man's conception of mind and personality almost to the breaking point. The atheist cannot believe that such an idea is possible. The theist goes as far as he can in imagining it, and then gives up, in faith that God is greater than our minds can possibly grasp. At this point the necessary agnosticism of the finite in the presence of the infinite must be acknowledged. Theists do not claim to know much; they merely believe that they are thinking along the right lines.

The German philosopher, Hans Vaihinger, once wrote a book entitled, *Die Philosophie des Als Ob* (*The Philosophy of As If*), which was popularized in England by Havelock Ellis. He makes a strong case for acting *as if* certain things are true, and argues that the nearest to the ultimate truth of certain ideas we can get is the verification that comes in thought and life when we act *as if* they were true, and enjoy the results.

No one need point out the dangers of such a philosophical form of pragmatism; but many scientists have affirmed its value in actual experimentation. One experiments *as if* a certain hypothesis were true; if the experiment works, the hypothesis is accepted as "true" in so far as its use in that particular type of experiment is concerned. Of course sometimes, as in the case of light, two different "as ifs" both seem to "work." In one type of experiment, light is treated as if it consisted of wave-motions, and in the other, as if it were an actual lightning-like forward movement of infinitesimal particles. The results of both types of experiment may be true *as far as they go;* each experiment may be valid within its own frame of reference.

The theist, in the Hebrew-Christian tradition, prays *as if*

God "hears" and "understands" and "loves" him. All down through the ages, men have testified to a feeling of communion and confrontation which became a conviction that the Divine *was* with them and that they *were* understood, challenged and forgiven. But an experience of this sort seems to depend on the belief that God is present. That is, one cannot have a very vivid religious experience if he thinks that he is merely apostrophizing: attributing personality to something essentially impersonal; the *as if* principle does not carry quite this far. But it *is* valid when one recognizes his finiteness, and sends his faith into the unknown in the belief that he is on the right track and not in a blind alley. Theodore Parker's biographer writes that in Dr. Parker's theology "God was a reality transcending distinctions of personal and impersonal" whereas in his devotions "God was as personal as his own father and mother and he prayed to him as such." That phrase "transcending distinctions of personal and impersonal" reminds us of Tillich's God as "being-itself," but for Dr. Parker to pray as if God were as "personal as his own father and mother," his theological conception must have been *beyond* and *above* any limiting qualifications associated with personality rather than *below* in the realm of the merely impersonal.

But the philosophical theist's faith is that God is infinite, not to be grasped in his totality by finite mind. There is a deep strain of agnosticism that conditions intelligent religious faith. Isaiah makes God say, "As the heavens are higher than the earth, so are my ways higher than your ways and my thoughts than your thoughts." Paul writes, "How unsearchable are God's judgments, and his ways past finding out." Martineau writes, "Our conception of God can never *correspond with reality* so as to be without omission, distortion or aberration, but can only *represent the reality* and stand for God within our souls." W. H. Auden in *Making and Judging Poetry* says, "Man is an analogy-drawing animal: that is his great good fortune. His danger is of treating analogies as identities."

Therefore, let us be careful of the terms we employ. Let us try to understand the meaning of what we say when we pray. We should be able to use the fine old Biblical terms for God if we are aware of how figurative and poetical they are. We do not have to take the Bible *literally* in order to take it *seriously*. When we take the imaginary compass-needle inside our minds, forcibly point it in the direction of atheism, and then let go, it may sometimes seem to linger there until we have explored the meaning of that view of life thoroughly and conscientiously. But if it does not satisfy us, if we feel that it is not really true, we will find the needle swinging back towards a spiritual interpretation of our existence. If then we pray to God as Father, in full recognition of both the glories and the limitations of that term, we may suddenly feel that he is with us, with his hand on our shoulder, and his still small voice whispering in our heart; and we may come to feel that he is personal because he seems to deal with us in personal communion as if each one of us were his only concern.

CHAPTER 3

The God of the Bible

WHAT we call gravity has probably been at work, in the same way it works now, ever since our planet solidified enough to have a crust. Solid objects, when dropped from a height, increase in speed thirty-two feet per second, if air-resistance is discounted; but if air-resistance is *not* discounted, it is obvious that a stone falls faster than a feather. Thus Aristotle arrived at the conclusion that heavier bodies fall more rapidly than lighter bodies. Well over nineteen hundred years later Galileo proved that it was air-resistance which accounted for the difference in the speed of falling, and not the difference in the mass of the objects. Now, in the age of earth-satellites, gravity is looked upon as an effect of our planetary magnetic field; but though man's understanding of this force has changed, and though his interpretation of its nature has altered, gravity itself has been reliably at work ever since our earth achieved its present size and stability.

When the Bible speaks of God as from "everlasting to everlasting," it means that the essential nature of the Divine has always been and always will be the same even though man's understanding has changed and, we believe, will continue to change and develop into something nearer to the truth. But there is a difference between the Christian's attitude towards man's clearer understanding of gravity, and of God. Gravity is an impersonal force, manifesting itself automatically when the conditions for its release are fulfilled; man's better grasp of its nature comes solely through his own efforts in theorizing, experimentation and verification. Only by the use of a form of apostrophizing could anyone say that gravity "reveals itself" to us. Surely we experience it; we have to come to terms with it; but we do not believe that it "speaks" to us, or "reveals" its nature to man; it is *we* who have to do the thinking that is necessary to arrive at a proper conclusion about it.

With God, the Christian feels the situation to be quite different. The Christian believes that somehow God takes the initiative. This does not mean that we can sit back and "receive" an adequate conception of the Divine without some active movement of thought or will or emotion on our part. We have a part to play in the reception of revelation. That part is both intellectual and moral: intellectual, in so far as our best thinking is necessary to clarify the nature of what is revealed, and make it an organic part of *all* our knowledge; moral, in so far as our commitment to the best we already know is the condition of our further understanding. This, of course, presupposes that God is in some sense "personal." As John Baillie says in his *The Idea of Revelation in Recent Thought,* "The course of nature is above all things impersonal. But God is personal, and a person can reveal Himself only through some kind of personal dealings with other persons." [1]

This, however, raises the question of why even sensitive, devout and committed "persons" seem to have "received" so much that is ambiguous and confusing, not to say contradictory. We "receptors" are conditioned by our education and culture, as well as by our personal differences and idiosyncracies. Practically, it often appears that the power we call God is in somewhat the same category as gravity: present and ready to operate when the proper conditions are fulfilled, but only to be understood by the self-initiated intellectual activity of man. And at this point, the evidence of the Bible is not completely conclusive.

Scholars seem fairly well agreed that the chief deity of the pre-Mosaic Hebrews was a mountain-god, though not localized in a way to prevent his being the ever-present, unseen chieftain of a tribe. All members of the tribe were considered kinsmen of the divine being. W. F. Albright believes that we can trace, among the early Hebrews, the recognition of "the right of an independent man or founder of a clan to choose his own personal God, with whom he is expected to enter into a kind of contractual relationship." [2] If this be true, the conditions were favorable for a spiritual giant like Moses to call God by a new name, and proclaim him and his covenant to the people. Albright argues with great subtlety that *Yahweh* means not only "I am what I am" but, if "transposed into the form of the third person required by the causative *Yahweh,*" can become *Yahweh asher Yihweh*, "He causes to be what comes into existence," in other words, *Creator.*[3]

Some of the remarks made about Yahweh indicate that, at first, he may have been thought of as attached to a certain locality: for instance, he had an encounter with Moses at Sinai, his base of operations. But also, very early, his dwelling-place was considered to be "heaven," and he could also be in the "Tabernacle" in the wilderness, and follow his children wherever they went, even unto the promised land. At first he was imagined to have a "body" of some sort, although this was usually hidden in what was spoken of as his "glory." In Exodus 33:23 Moses is reported to have seen his "back parts" but not his face, for no man could look upon Yahweh's face and live. This is not quite as anthropomorphic a conception as the deity who walked in the Garden of Eden in "the cool of the day" and from whom Adam foolishly thought he could hide; but it is still a long way from the God of the first chapter of Genesis, who created "the heavens and the earth." [4]

Yahweh is pictured as having emotions—human emotions on a heroic scale: love, hatred, joy, sorrow, revenge, remorse, all awe-inspiringly magnified. This conception made it possible for him to be conceived as deeply concerned about individuals, as well as about groups or tribes or nations. From the beginning of the Bible, he was thought to have a personal interest in the average Hebrew. Although, as Albright so well says, "There was in him (Yahweh) none of the human frailties that make the Olympian deities of Greece such charming poetic figures and such unedifying examples," [5] yet he was believed to enjoy the sacrifice of domestic animals and birds (cattle, sheep, goats, doves), which in pre-Mosaic religion had been for centuries a means of paying homage to a divinity, solemnizing important occasions, and cementing the relationship between worshippers and worshipped.

Yahweh also was conceived as promulgating a categorical code of observance and behavior, largely negative, but with far-reaching positive implications. Prohibitions of disloyalty, idolatry, sacrilege, Sabbath-violation, murder, adultery, theft, lying and greed were felt to be laid down by the deity, and not to be merely the results of accepted or codified common sense and prudence. Yahweh was imagined as *initiating* his relationship to the Israelites, of causing the burning of the bush to arrest Moses' attention, of speaking his name so that Moses could understand it and could proclaim it, of sending Moses back to Egypt to free his people, of hardening Pharaoh's heart and so trying the Hebrews in the fire of persecution, of sending the plagues and killing the first-born of the Egyptian children, of opening the Red Sea for the chosen people and closing it over the heads of their enemies. In response to these "mighty acts" of God, the Israelites, at their best, were grateful. In their exalted moments, they believed themselves to be children of the covenant. God had delivered them; God had promised them a land in which to live; God had given them a divinely inspired code of laws; God expected them to be loyal. And much of their subsequent history is phrased in terms of their disloyalty, the call of the prophets to repent of their defection, the punishment visited on them when they refused to listen, the defeat and dispersion of some, the exile of others; until Yahweh in his mercy restored a remnant of them for the rebuilding of his temple and the re-establishment of their national life. In all this, God is pictured as personally active on the grand scale.

The *Elohim* (God) of the Garden of Eden is not quite the same as the *Yahweh* of the Exodus or the *Elohim* who used Cyrus of Persia to end the Exile and return the faithful to Jerusalem. That is, the conception of God was greatly enlarged between the Fall and the Restoration. There are certain elements common to both, of course; he is personal, he is righteous, he is concerned for man; but there are some rather striking differences, too. From the God who interrogates Adam and Eve and the serpent, he became under the name of Yahweh subsequently, a storm God, a war God, a tribal God, often thought of as hating Israel's enemies, pleased by the slaughter of prisoners of war, and enjoying the sweet savor of the burning blood and fat of animal sacrifices. He was a primitive God compared with that of Jeremiah, to say nothing of the God of Jesus. After the conquest of Canaan, Yahweh became more of an agricultural deity, sometimes conceived as limited territorially, and thought of by a few as tolerating certain forms of fertility rites usually associated with Baal-worship.[6] There were always those who criticized this imitation of alien religious practices, and it is from those who were scandalized that we learn of the scandals.

True monotheism was a long time in coming. It seems to have taken the wider experience of foreign contacts, the elevated thought-patterns of the writing prophets, and the deepening piety of truly religious Hebrews to stretch the concept to embrace genuine universality. Yahweh was thought of as the God of the sky, then of the heavens above the sky; the deity of more than Canaan, then the Power which used all known nations for his purposes. And possibly even more important than this, Yahweh was increasingly believed to be *ethical,* concerned about man's treatment of man, the Israelites' treatment of the wanderer and the sojourner, the treatment of the poor by the rich, the treatment of women by men. Amos insisted that God is a God of justice; Hosea developed the idea that *Elohim* is also a God of mercy; Isaiah stressed the unutterable holiness of the deity; and Micah summed up these three ideas, maybe without meaning to do so, in the justly famous sentence: "He hath showed thee, O man, what is good; and what doth the Lord require of thee, but to do justly, and to love mercy, and to walk humbly with thy God?" [7]

Hosea could liken Israel's disloyalty to God to a "whoredom" [8] on her part. His own wife's faithlessness probably suggested the figure; and yet the prophet continued to love his mate even in her faithlessness. Hosea was sure that God continued to love Israel in spite of her infidelity. God was Israel's "husband"; *he* had always been faithful; it was the Hebrew people who had been false. The nature of the defection was twofold: Israel had been untrue to the moral commandments of the Law and the principles of human charity and kindness; Israel had also been untrue to the *worship* of God by following the immoral practices associated with heathen ritual, sometimes even importing these practices into the worship of Yahweh himself; furthermore, even though many followed the *forms* of Yahweh-worship, they substituted ritual observance for ethical behavior.

Amos had spelled out the violations of social justice which Hosea interpreted as part of Israel's "whoredom." Amos made God thunder against those who felt "at ease in Zion," "secure in the mountain of Samaria." The rich people whiled the day away on "beds of ivory," eating the "lambs out of the flock," singing "idle songs" to the accompaniment of seductive stringed instruments, anointing themselves with exotic perfumes, and drinking their wine from "bowls." They oppressed "the poor" and crushed "the needy," and yet they sponsored the most elaborate possible services, "assemblies" and sacrifices. But God, said Amos, would not accept these offerings. He hated and "despised" their feasts; he "took no delight" in the "solemn assemblies"; he would not accept the "burnt-offerings" and the "meal-offerings" or the "peace offerings" of their "fat beasts." He did not even enjoy the music, because it proceeded from a people licentious and hard of heart. The only things that would satisfy him were "judgment" and "righteousness."

Hosea made God call for "mercy" among men, consideration of the rich for the poor, rather than "sacrifice," and a true knowledge of him "more than burnt offerings."

Of course, Hosea suggested that God's heart could be moved by repentance; God was ready to forgive; he could not easily "give up" Ephraim or "cast off" Israel. Yet the people did not repent; the Assyrians defeated and scattered the northern tribes; the Babylonians conquered Assyria and took Judah captive; and the Exiles then had the better part of half a century in a "strange land" to lick their wounds, meditate on their fate, gather the precious documents of their history and faith together, and try to prepare themselves for what God might have in store for them by way of an eventual restoration.

In the towering figure of Jeremiah, all the pre-Exilic prophesies of Amos, Hosea, Isaiah, Micah and the rest came to magnificent fruition. In his thought, Yahweh was the master of history, the sovereign of all nations, the ethical ruler of the world. "Do I not fill heaven and earth?" he makes God ask. For him it was not necessary actually to *worship* other gods in order to "serve" them; merely to be unrighteous, was in itself, infidelity. The unknown prophet, whom we call the Second Isaiah, filled out this conception with his eloquent and winsome poetry: "Before me no god was formed, nor shall there be any after me"; [9] "I am the first and I am the last; besides me there is no god." [10] The Exile convinced the more thoughtful Hebrews that Yahweh was chastising them for their defection from him, and yet they treasured the hope that he would give them another chance. All at once, Cyrus defeated the Babylonians and granted the Exiles their opportunity. Many of them returned to settle in what was left of Jerusalem. First under Zerubbabel, and later under Nehemiah, the walls were rebuilt and the Temple worship re-established. Well could Nehemiah claim, when some saboteurs tried to interrupt him, "I am doing a great work, and I cannot come down." [11]

As Fosdick points out, in Judaism, as in all living religions, we find contradictions between prophets and people, between one author and another, one tradition and the next. "Post Exilic Judaism . . . presents in its theology a profound variance—monotheism, taken morally in earnest, mingled with old ideas involved in tribal deities, racial prejudices, religious bigotries, and national hatreds." [12] We have on one side the Book of Esther, revealing the "fiery heart of Jewish nationalism in the third century B.C.," and, on the other side, the books of Ruth and Jonah. Yahweh seems cruel at one time, kindhearted at another. Isaiah writes, "In that day shall Israel be the third with Egypt and with Assyria, a blessing in the midst of the earth; for that Yahweh of hosts hath blessed them, saying, blessed be Egypt my people, and Assyria the work of my hands, and Israel mine inheritance"; [13] but the Second Isaiah writes, in a spirit which seems somewhat like a lapse on his part, that the kings and queens of the world will "bow down to thee (Israel) with their faces to the earth, and lick the dust of thy feet." [14] In Zechariah's prophecy we find the contrast included in one conception, "Yahweh shall be king over all the earth: in that day shall Yahweh be one, and his name one," [15] and "Whoso of all the families of the earth goeth not up to Jerusalem to worship the King, Yahweh of hosts, upon them shall there be no *rain.*" [16]

It often stretches the modern minister's acknowledgment of the symbolic nature of religious language to the breaking-point when he reads a scripture lesson from an inspiring book only to find, side by side with something to which he can say a grateful "Amen," something else which he simply cannot believe, even taken symbolically. Nor is it a matter of the Hebrew names of God, one universally signifying a certain concept and another meaning something else. *We* use the words *God,* the *Lord,* or *Jehovah* to translate *el, elah, elohim, eloah, yahweh, yah, tsur;* and know that *our* words for the Divine cover different concepts. But the case is complicated by the fact that just as there are contrasting conceptions *within* our terms, so are there *within* the Hebrew terms themselves. As we have seen, *Elohim* may be used for a very primitive concept or for an advanced one; *Yahweh* is thought of as tribal at one time, universal at another.

What happens is that the believer phrases his understanding of the Divine in terms of the highest values he can conceive at the moment and within his particular frame of reference. His sense of communion with God involves a *confrontation* which challenges him to hear and obey. But God does not dictate the *terms* in which this sense of communion will be described; the terms a man uses to make his faith articulate will depend on his vocabulary, his concerns, his historical situation. Samson will differ from Samuel in this regard, David from Hosea, Elijah from Ezekiel, the shepherd from the soldier, the subject from the ruler. The same man may emphasize one aspect of the Divine at one time and another at another; and a devout soul who lived a thousand years before Christ will, though in the same tradition, think and speak of God differently from one who lived nine hundred years later. And yet, in one sense all are "worshipping the same God." At least, according to our faith, the one and the same God is graciously shedding his light upon our existence; different stained glass windows transmit differing amounts of that light to the dark interior of life's cathedral. The windows vary in beauty and brilliance, but without the light they would not glow at all. We cannot push this analogy to its logical conclusion, but it may be suggestive of the point I wish to make.

A humble subject, to whom an oriental potentate represents the acme of personal power and dignity, will feel he is honoring God by thinking of him as "King of Kings and Lord of Lords," the "King of Glory," the "Great King above all Gods." A grateful warrior will thank the deity for strength to defend his people, and speak reverently of a "God of hosts," a "Lord mighty in battle," who "teaches" the soldier's hands to war, who breaks the enemies of Israel "with a rod of iron," and "dashes them in pieces like a vessel." God is his "shield and buckler," the "lifter up of his head," who "smites" his enemies upon the cheek-bone, and breaks "the teeth of the ungodly." [17]

At other times in Scripture, God is spoken of as acting *maternally*, "As one whom a mother comforts, so I will comfort you," [18] or *paternally*, "As a father pities his children, so the Lord pities those who fear him." [19] A favorite analogy is that of *Shepherd*, but God is also thought of as speaking to Moses as one *friend* would speak to another.[20] Hosea thinks of him as a *Bridegroom*,[21] Jeremiah as a *Husband*.[22] And so, although there is a wide spectrum of descriptive similes and metaphors employed in the Old Testament, some early, some late, some inadequate if not misleading, others inspiring and helpful, post-Exilic Judaism is ready for the next stage of revelation. For at its best, the conception of God in the Psalms and the Prophets is the basis for the teaching of Jesus.

I have heard uninformed preachers speak as if the God of the Old Testament were chiefly a God of wrath, or at least merely of Justice and Judgment, whereas the God of the New Testament were exclusively a God of Love and

Mercy. This is not a true way of phrasing the difference. The God of *both* Testaments is one of both Justice *and* Mercy. So is the best type of earthly father. He loves his children, but he will not spoil them. He forgives them when they fail but does not make light of sin. Most of the Psalms contain both elements. Psalm 1 stresses the blessedness of the man who delights in the law of the Lord, but the law must be observed if he wishes to be "like a tree planted by the rivers of water." Psalm 19 emphasizes the way in which the heavens declare God's glory; he is the creator and sustainer of all things; his ordinances are righteous, his fear is clean, he is a *loving* Judge. Psalm 24 pictures the King of Glory, who wants men to be worthy of standing in his presence, with clean hands and pure hearts; the Lord then will bless and vindicate his children. Psalm 103 shows him as forgiving, healing, redeeming, crowning, satisfying; he is slow to anger and plenteous in mercy; his righteousness is upon those who fear him, who keep his covenant, and who remember to obey his commandments. Psalm 139 sings that we cannot get away from God, no matter how hard we try, and beseeches him to search and understand and lead man in the way everlasting. Righteousness and mercy are woven together as warp and woof in these Psalms.

It is true that in some Psalms the *sterner* aspects of the deity are stressed almost to the exclusion of the more gracious and winsome; [23] whereas in some of the best loved Psalms the *kindlier* aspects are set forth to the exclusion of the less appealing; [24] but in general both conceptions are like the loci of an ellipse, and the elliptical form is necessary to set forth the conception adequately.

It is not true that Jesus' teaching about God represents nothing but the winsome and appealing aspects of the divine nature. God is *primarily* love; but he is also *stern* towards the hard of heart. He forgives, but he will not, nay he cannot, forgive those who do not forgive others. It were better that a millstone be hanged about a man's neck rather than that he should cause a "little one" to sin.[25] Those who do not minister to others when they are hungry, thirsty, friendless, naked, sick and imprisoned are condemned to "eternal punishment" in the fire prepared for the devil and his angels.[26] Granting the figurative and even hyperbolic character of some of Jesus' phraseology, it is still quite clear that the early Church, through whom we receive our knowledge of Christ, taught that Jesus' conception was of a God of Judgment as well as of Mercy.

When the followers of Christ were expelled from the synagogues and the temple because they preached that the Messiah had already come, some new features began to creep into their thoughts about God. Under the leadership of Paul, the converted Pharisee, the promises of the Old Testament were acknowledged as having been fulfilled. Jesus of Nazareth was none other than the Christ. The rejection of this concept by most of the Jews sent the "Christiani" out into the Graeco-Roman world to bring the "Good News" to the Gentiles. The earliest letter of Paul which survives shows the definite beginnings of a conception of God which is more than undifferentiated monotheism of the type held by, say, Jeremiah or the Second Isaiah. In First Thessalonians, Paul speaks of the converts as having been "chosen" by God, as being "imitators" of "Christ," living with a "joy inspired by the Holy Spirit." Now that Jesus Christ has come and lived and died and risen again, so that to be "in him" is to feel the power of the Divine in one's heart and soul, the activity of God as Creator, Redeemer and Sustainer seems too complex to be taken care of by one undifferentiated deity, no matter how many absolute qualities he is thought to possess. Jesus becomes "the Lord." The "Holy Ghost" or "Holy Spirit" is also operative. Sometimes, "the Lord is the Spirit"; but it is all God at work; no theologian had as yet tried to phrase or think through a conception of a trinity. The intimate experience of God in Christ as an ever-present joyful reality had not yet been defined as One God in Three Persons.

It would be fascinating and instructive if we could get back of the records of the first three Gospels and have a stenographic transcript of what Jesus actually said when he was on earth, translated into idiomatic English; but it is possible that his teaching about God would not be very different from what we now have. There are strong reasons for believing that the kind of teaching he gave could be transmitted with remarkable accuracy through an oral tradition. He taught by means of parables, epigrams, arresting figures of speech, all easily memorable, especially to those who were so impressed by him that they testified to his speaking "as never man spake." He called the Deity *abba Father, our Father,* but mostly just *your Father, thy Father, my Father* or simply *God.* He attributed to him the qualities of goodness, perfection, mercy, holiness, unity, knowledge and wisdom, love towards the lost, kindness, patience, and omnipotence: these are the characteristics which we should hold in mind as we pray, "Our Father which art in heaven." All the parables of Jesus are but illustrations of this conception; all his epigrammatic statements merely throw light on one or another of these attributes; even the hyperbole is explicable in terms of a Father who is all in all ("with God all things are possible"). There is nothing here but a universalizing of what the Old Testament writers, in their moments of highest inspiration, taught about Yahweh. But Jesus impressed his most intimate followers with the *vivid-*

ness of his intimacy with the Father, as well as with his *utter fidelity* to that relationship. The idea of his sinlessness must have come from this. Although the Nazarene himself replied to a sycophant who addressed him as "Good Master," "Why callest thou me good? There is none good but one, that is, God," [27] his very life convinced his followers that he was "without sin." [28]

When the first century was far spent, the author of the Fourth Gospel attributed to Jesus many statements which are in marked contrast to the *style* and *form* of his teaching in Matthew, Mark and Luke. But the *content* can be interpreted as a perfectly defensible extension or adaptation of the earlier ideas to meet the needs of a new generation. God is *God* or *my Father;* he is a spirit, invisible, glorified in his Son; his word is true, he is completely reliable. The most marvellously characteristic and most frequently quoted sentence from the Johannine teaching is, "God so loved the world that he gave his only begotten Son, that whosoever believeth in him should not perish but have everlasting life." [29] And then Jesus is made to continue, speaking in the third person, "For God sent not his Son into the world to condemn the world; but that the world through him might be saved." [30]

Jesus is therefore thought of as God's Son in a very special sense. The Fourth Gospel goes far beyond the first three in elaborating just what this means. The Father and the Son are known best only by the other.[31] The Father is "in" the Son and the Son "in" the Father.[32] They are "one," [33] and yet in some real way, the Father is "greater" than the Son.[34] Christ can do "nothing" of himself,[35] but was appointed to do his Father's work [36] and to be his spokesman.[37]

The Gospel of John begins with a statement which surely introduces new dimensions into the concept of Christ; he is now thought of as *the Word, the Logos.* The idea of the Logos—the activity of God in creation and salvation—was not unfamiliar to many at the time the Gospel was written; the unfamiliar idea would have been the identification of that Logos with Christ—a pre-existent Christ. This is surely another step in the development of the trinitarian thinking which was eventually systematized in the great creeds. The Fourth Gospel begins with the Pre-existent Word, which is the agent of Creation, the Source of life and light, and the One who appears on the human stage, "the Word made flesh," as Jesus the Christ. God the Father is the *ground* of the Divine; the *Comforter* is the Holy Spirit who will be sent to minister to men after Christ is taken away from them; but by that time the Deity will be thought of as an awe-inspiring, ontological triumvirate—one God, the richness of whose life cannot, however, be thought of in terms simply of an undifferentiated unitary Person. It was to be some time before the theologians would attempt to give precision to this concept, but by the end of the Johannine period the materials for such a concept were at hand, based on the imaginative interpretation of vivid personal religious experience.

In Paul's teaching, "It is God, that said, Light shall shine out of darkness, who shined in our hearts, to give the light the knowledge of the glory of God in the face of Jesus Christ." [38] Jesus becomes the "image of God." [39] God the Father becomes spiritually a *Christlike* God. This foreshadows John's affirmation of a Christ who could say, "He that hath seen me hath seen the Father." [40] Although in the first three Gospels God is never given the *attribute of love directly* (except love for the "lost"), in the Fourth Gospel he is pictured as *loving the world,* and in the Johannine

Epistles we find the memorable statement, "*God is love;* and he that abideth in love abideth in God, and God abideth in him." [41]

And so the Bible's earliest image of the Divine is a manlike being, with a body of sorts, who "walks" and "talks" and interrogates, and is afraid that man will eat of the fruit of the tree of life and become as he is. Later we have a "storm God on a desert mountain," a tribal God of battles, a God limited in his jurisdiction to the territory of his chosen people. Ethically, the God of the Old Testament sometimes offends us with his sanction of the massacre of Israel's enemies; and yet we suddenly are aware that as man grows in ethical discrimination and moral vision the concept of God also grows into the Deity of all the world who desires man to walk before him in righteousness, mercy and humility. It is the Christian's faith that God has been trying to reveal his true nature to man from the very beginning, but that this true nature could not be comprehended, with anything like adequacy, by nomads fighting for their life through hostile territory on the way to a "promised land." The land is finally conquered, a settled agricultural life exacts its peculiar toll, a civil war occurs, prosperity brings comforts but also evils in its wake, tolerance of foreign cults weakens the strictness of religious devotion; the prophets see the trouble, pronounce their judgment, but their message falls upon deaf ears; Israel is scattered, Judah is captured, and then, in humility and exile, the seers begin to understand the meaning of the people's hardships. God gives them another chance; and the idea of the Father, seen more clearly by the few, constitutes the basis for revelation in the Son, who becomes the "image of God." God is now *Christlike,* though infinite and universal. His power is overwhelming but his nature is essentially love; man's imagination has shot its most daring surmise into the unknown as a response to the best it has experienced in Jesus; and thus Christian theology is born.

CHAPTER 4

The God of Our Tradition

LET US consider the various ways in which the God of the Bible, who begins as a limited man-like being and ends as the Father of our Lord Jesus Christ, was thought to reveal his will to men, his concrete desires as to the ordering of their affairs. Although it is impossible to call them completely distinct modes of communication, they *are* separable in thought. The first has to do with the way God is believed to have spoken *directly* to the great spiritual leaders of Israel: "He made known his ways unto Moses," "And the Lord spake unto Moses face to face." Most of the seers and prophets felt that they had received direct, unique, unmistakable messages from God, which they often tried to refuse or resist, but to which they were eventually obedient. They did not think of themselves, nor were they thought of, as "creative" individuals. They did not consider their knowledge as due to what we now describe as intuition or insight. They were simply *obedient men* to whom God had revealed himself in a unique way. When they obeyed, and spoke what had been revealed, more often than not they came into open conflict with society, and even with some of the pious people of their time. It was usually in retrospect that Israel pronounced favorably upon the authenticity of their messages. If they had been asked to frame a theory of divine guidance, they would have responded very simply: the Controller of Israel's Destiny (and, in the later prophets, the Ruler of All Nations) had come to them with such vividness, had spoken to them with such irresistible inner authority, that even the words of fellow human beings seemed less certain to them than the Divine Voice. Yahweh had a declaration to make; he wished to make it through them; it had to do with the salvation of his people, which was his eternal concern. They were bothered by no intellectual problems about whether or not it were possible for God to reveal himself; their concern was with their own unworthiness or immaturity or unfitness to receive the revelation.

The way God was conceived as making his will known to the rank and file was *through* the prophets and the lawgivers, and through the *interpretation* of inspired pronouncements and codes. The extent to which anything like a direct divine communication was granted to the average Israelite varies from period to period. Yet Yahweh was always acknowledged as present and in control of life. Isaiah, for example, would not have expected others to have the same tremendous commissions that he received, yet he was ever anxious that men and women be aware of God and his activity in the world. There were times when any blunt assertion that the ordinary individual could receive *direct* divine guidance would have been resisted as dangerous to the faith, as opening up too many avenues for the expression of the vagaries of the undisciplined. There were all sorts of "false prophets" claiming private revelations; and quite often the prophets of Yahweh denounced them because their utterances lacked that strong ethical note which was the hallmark of inspiration. So a genuine distinction was made between the spiritual leaders who experienced an unmediated revelation and the great mass of devout folk who lived by faith in God as given to the community through the prophets.

As time went on, however, the increasing emphasis upon the solicitude of God for his people, coupled with the growing conception of individual moral responsibility, made the development of personal piety logical and necessary. Ordinary experience came to be interpreted in religious terms. Although emotionalism was looked upon with suspicion, there is a warmth of expression in the Psalms which exhibits faith in a merciful God who guides his people. Although at least five separate Hebrew words are translated "guide" in the Old Testament (*darak, yaats, nahag, nahal,* and *nachah*), the emphasis in all of them is on the solicitous activity of Yahweh: "The meek will he *guide* in judgment; and the meek will he teach his way." [1] "I will instruct thee and teach thee in the way which thou shalt go; I will *guide* thee with mine eye." [2] In the spirit of this intimate relationship between God and his people, the *past* could be interpreted: "But he made his own people to go forth like sheep, and *guided* them in the wilderness like a flock." [3] "The Lord . . . *guided* them on every side." [4] The *future* is also in the hands of God: "For this God is our God for ever and ever; he will be our *guide* even unto death." [5] The much beloved Twenty-third Psalm suggests some sort of direct guidance of our footsteps by Yahweh.

The Old Testament is filled with references to *angels* who made God's purposes known to men. We might consider this a separate explanation of guidance, as would also be the revelation of God's will in dreams and in visions. Still another mode is suggested in I Samuel 28:6: "And when Saul enquired of the Lord, the Lord answered him not, neither by dreams, nor by *Urim,* nor by prophets." Urim is mentioned along with Thummin as something in the high priests' breastplate that gave an oracular response. Here we are plunged into *divination* which, in its cruder forms, was a vestigial remainder from a naive animistic period and which can be traced back to where it becomes lost in the mists of pre-history. As religion becomes more ethical, the purely magical aspects of man's relation to superhuman powers tend to fade into the background. The prophets were often vehement in their denunciation of divination as leading men astray. Isaiah speaks in no uncertain terms, "And when they shall say unto you, Seek unto them that have familiar spirits, and unto wizards that peep and that mutter; should not a people seek unto their God?" [6] So, although prophetic revelation, the interpretation of prophecy and law, the direct guidance of the pious by a Divine Shepherd, as well as divinely inspired dreams, visions, oracles and angels, may all be thought of as separate methods of communication, it is "God who worketh," and for the truly religious soul that was the central fact.

Of course, a distinction should be drawn between *conscious* and *unconscious* guidance of life by God. Because the writers of the later Psalms believed in Yahweh's ever-present activity, they felt that for the reverent soul *all* leadings which were ethical and spiritual in character were from God, even though they would hardly have claimed special, immediate, and unique divine illumination. Even the great seers distinguished between the direct and indirect leading of God. Elijah did not find God in the wind, or the earthquake, or the fire, but in "the still small voice," yet he was perfectly prepared to find him manifested in any or all of these. Had God been in any other than what J. A.

Bewer called the "quivering silence," it would simply have been a confirmation of the belief that God can speak as and how he chooses. The Wisdom literature is full of suggestions as to the more direct method of communication. Wisdom is represented as God saying: "I will make known my ways unto you." [7] It is against the background of this attitude towards the Divine that we can understand the New Testament conceptions of divine guidance.

Jesus was nourished in the traditions of Judaism. He shared its religious interpretation of Life. The development of his own feeling that he was under God's guidance may have come gradually as he increased in wisdom, and stature, and in favor with God and man, but it is also possible that the clear conviction of his unique mission occurred to him in a flash, or in all series of sudden illuminations. The encounter with John the Baptist was the occasion of one such striking experience. This is indicated by the account in Mark of Jesus' vision of the dove at baptism, his consciousness of the approval of God, and his retreat to the wilderness to think out the meaning of it all for his life. That he rejected the strategy of armed revolution is seen by some commentators in what must have been his account to his disciples of the third temptation.[8] The first two temptations (in the order presented in Matthew) can be interpreted as a rejection of any attempt to convince the world of the validity of his message by mere wonder-working, devoid of ethical significance.[9] We cannot tell how far the Master himself went in his belief in Satan, unclean spirits, angels and the like. The early Church believed in them, and believed that Christ believed in them. We are on very uncertain ground when we try to get back of the records to his own personal convictions in the matter, but we surely can be certain that he believed in the direct guidance of the Holy Spirit (God as an Active Presence), in his own dependence upon his heavenly Father, and in his commission to utter both a promise and a warning—a promise of the good news of the kingdom, and a warning that those who were unworthy to share its blessing would be condemned and cast out.

The only place in the first three Gospels where Jesus mentioned the *Spirit* in connection with his *mission* was in self-defence, when the Pharisees declared that he could expel evil spirits only because he collaborated with Satan.[10] Jesus said that he was thus empowered by the Holy Spirit, which represented God's activity in working to overthrow the reign of Satan. Luke used the figurative expression, "the Finger of God," for the "Holy Spirit" in the parallel passage in the Third Gospel. It is likely that Christ's consciousness of being continually used by God prompted the difficult saying that blasphemy against the Holy Spirit was beyond pardon.[11]

References to the *Spirit* in Jesus' teaching are rare. In Mark 13:11 we read: "But when they shall . . . deliver you up, take no thought beforehand what ye shall speak, neither do ye premeditate, but whatsoever shall be given you in that hour, that speak ye; for it is not ye that speak, but the Holy Ghost." The Spirit, in the first three Gospels, was promised as a special equipment for emergencies.

In some ways it is strange that we do not find a clearer emphasis upon divine guidance in the teaching of Jesus; much was made of it in primitive Christianity. But we know that Christ assumed many things which he did not mention, or upon which he did not lay particular emphasis. He assumed the reality of God's continuous activity in life; he spent much time in prayer, and was careful to indicate what he thought was an important distinction between "vain repetitions" and real communion. He obviously expected to get not only reinforcement but guidance from God in his early morning meditations on the hilltops. And his spiritual struggle in the garden of Gethsemane was resolved when he felt it to be God's will that he drink the bitter cup of a criminal's death.

Although the precise nature of Jesus' messianic consciousness is still in doubt and may always be in doubt, it does not seem far-fetched to assume that he had a sense of a personal relationship to God that was different from that of his followers. We have seen how a prophet like Isaiah was aware that God had singled him out above others to be the bearer of a special message; but he would also believe that God had ways of making his will known to the humblest man whose attitude was right. Orthodox Christianity has always taught that Jesus' relationship to God was more completely and continuously intimate than that of even the greatest prophets; he is felt to be in a class absolutely by himself. The prophets, in their turn, had a kind of guidance not vouchsafed to the ordinary man; the New Testament apostles had a special measure of divine power and direction. But our faith has always acknowledged the possibility of every converted soul's being guided in some very real way by the active Spirit of God in Christ.

After the death and resurrection of Jesus, two marked changes, already mentioned, took place: the development of the view that Jesus was not only the Messiah but the Divine Son of God, and that he came to define the *character* not only of the Father but the Spirit. Jesus was thought of as God's Son in a *unique* sense; men who believed in him were also *sons;* but now it was not men in general who were sons but those who acknowledged Christ. Christ was the only *divine* Son. Paul suggested that God is to be thought of not merely in *personal* terms but in terms of "*substance*," "essence," essential being; this essential being can be shared by more than one *person;* Christ shares his Father's "essence," and the Christian also, in some measure, can share the divine nature. God, active as the Spirit, also shares this essential being, the moral attributes of which are defined by Christ. So Paul taught that God was manifesting himself as an active Presence, identified at times as the *alter ego* of the risen Jesus, who guided men specifically and directly. "While Peter thought on the vision, the Spirit said unto him, Behold, three men seek thee. Arise, therefore, and get thee down, and go with them, doubting nothing, for I have sent them." [12] The Spirit told Philip to approach the Ethiopian eunuch,[13] would not let Paul and Timothy go into Bithynia,[14] guided Paul to plan a trip to Rome.[15] The Holy Ghost is spoken of as witnessing in every city.[16] Sometimes the will of God is made known in *visions:* as when the Lord appeared to Ananias, and when Paul saw the man from Macedonia. Sometimes an *angel* appeared with a message, or a "man in bright clothing." But whatever the particular manifestation, or the term used, or the descriptive words employed, God was felt to be behind it all; *his* Spirit was actively at work.

Tradition has it that this same Spirit filled a group of believers *fully* for the first time at Pentecost; the evidence of the divine activity at that moment was a vibrant spiritual experience, and a miraculous speaking in foreign tongues. Some of the uninitiated who were present accused the disciples of being full of new wine! Peter, however, rose to their defence, and connected this ecstatic visitation both with the prophecy of Joel and with the resurrection of Christ. But the Spirit proved to be, especially in the view of Paul, not mainly productive of ecstatic experience, but of moral integrity and spiritual insight; and such direct guidance as the Spirit gave always had reference to a religious task of some sort.

In the later Johannine view, the guidance of the Spirit, in a specifically Christian sense, was not available until *after* Jesus had risen. Jesus had been with men for a few years in the flesh. He had borne witness to the power of God both in his teaching, which others could follow then and there, and in his own person, which made upon men a unique impression of authority and strength. But the new dispensation began in earnest with his ascension and glorification. All the fresh and vital intuitions, insights, and experiences of the spiritually abundant life were the work of the "*Paracletos*," of which our word "Comforter" is an inadequate translation. The Spirit as Paraclete operated to enlighten men as to the real nature of Christ. The Spirit of Truth, a synonym for Paraclete, was however confined to the operation of the Spirit in the community. There was every reason to believe that the Spirit would continue to to reveal more and more truth to men as they were able to receive it. Although there is very little intimation, in the Johannine literature, of the Spirit's giving specific guidance on practical matters, there is nothing in the Fourth Gospel or the Epistles of John to preclude such a possibility.

It has often been noted that there is a rather striking contrast between the teaching of Jesus in the first three Gospels about man's nature, and the teaching of the Church. Jesus seemed to base his message on the belief that God had given to man a nature capable of both good and evil. Leaving aside the problem of Christ's sinlessness, no one was *completely* good, and possibly no one completely evil; but there were people whom Jesus himself called good and others whom he called evil. The good were those who believed in God and were trying to do his will. The bad were those living in sin and pride, and who were not doing God's will. The good would be saved; the bad, punished. Towards the end of Jesus' ministry, his increasing sense of mission led him to identify God's cause with his own cause, in the sense that those who followed him and believed as he did were considered on the side of the Father.[17]

The difference between this view and that of later Christianity is not so much a conflict of conviction as a contrast in approach. The matrix of thought in which Jesus lived and worked was Hebraic; the matrix of thought in the Graeco-Roman world was Hellenistic. Greek speculation about the nature of the universe had taken many forms, but one line of reasoning was particularly important for religion: a sharp separation was made between the visible material world and the invisible spiritual world. The soul of man was conceived as something divine, which really belonged to a higher sphere, but which had come to be imprisoned in a fleshly body. The idea was held in a refined and sophisticated form by the neo-Platonists; it was also the basis, in other forms, for the so-called mystery-religions. Along with it went a craving of salvation, a yearning for the deliverance of the soul from its material prison, a longing here and now for escape from man's continual slavery to bodily passions and appetites, and an intense desire for a life beyond death. Material things were bad; spiritual things were good.

When Christianity came to deal with these conceptions, it adopted or adapted them, insisted that they be regarded from the ethical point of view, and worked out a theory of salvation in terms of them. One can see how the idea that human nature is *essentially* corrupt, that is, corrupt in its very essence, could gain wide acceptance among Gentile

Christians and those familiar with Greek thought; it represented, in its Christian form, a fusion of the neo-Platonic doctrine of the worthlessness of the flesh with the Hebrew notion of the heinousness of sin, meriting the just wrath of God. Sin seemed to be an evidence not only of ethical waywardness, but of metaphysical corruption. Mere will-power was incapable of leading to self-control; redemption had to be from *outside* and *above* or *beyond* the material realm.

The acceptance of this Hellenistic approach by Christendom had far-reaching results. It led to the pursuit of a certain type of mysticism, in the realization of which the divine nature was thought of as flowing into and redeeming human nature. In Paul's thought, a strong emphasis was placed on the ethical fruits of redemption; the person into whom the divine life flowed became guided by the Holy Spirit; and the fruits of the Spirit were "love, joy, peace, longsuffering, gentleness, goodness, faith, meekness and temperance." [18]

This Christianity offered salvation of a spiritual sort, a powerful indwelling divine life, and a Lord far more compelling and ethically satisfying than the "lords" of the mystery-cults. Yet there were elements in the Gospel which repelled some. The Jews could not bring themselves to believe that Jesus of Nazareth was the promised Messiah; those of a Gnostic temper of mind could not conceive of a Divine Son suffering the torture of crucifixion; the challenge to live a life of sobriety, purity, simplicity and charity was too much for the worldlings. The preaching of Christ crucified was, therefore, "unto the Jews a stumbling-block and unto the Greeks foolishness." Maybe, said some, the body of Jesus was unreal, and his sufferings an illusion by which the malignant spirits who ruled this world had been deceived; the Docetists reasoned thus. Others said that the Divine Being who dwelt in the body of Jesus, along with his human spirit, left that body and returned to heaven before the passion, so that only Jesus the man suffered.

To combat these, and other interesting but perverse theories, an appeal was made to those whose authority was derived from the teachers of the first generation; these leaders responded manfully. They placed the seal of their approval on certain of the writings which were being circulated, and denied approval to others; so that, by the end of the second century the Four Gospels, the Acts, the Epistles of Paul, I Peter and I John were accepted as undeniably representing the Christian way of thought and life, with a number of other books accepted in some places though not elsewhere. The Church of Rome and its presiding bishop were appealed to as authorities, showing their recognized importance. Thus, to protect the purity of the Gospel, the Christian fellowship was forced to assert itself against heretics, consolidate its organization, decide its canon of Scripture, and later to define its creeds. There must be *not churches,* but *a Church.* The Gnostics were excluded, yet Christianity had to come to grips with Greek philosophy; and in Clement of Alexandria and Origen the Church produced two theologians who began the tremendous intellectual task of thinking through the implications of the faith in terms of the noblest philosophy then known.

Naturally, the central problem was the relation of God to Christ. Christianity inherited from Judaism a strong monotheistic tendency; yet many early believers made Christ their God, and did not concern themselves with the divine creation and government of the universe, or the connection of Christ with the supreme Deity. They were primarily interested in salvation, and as "Lord" of their "cult," Christ was able to guarantee that. As time went on, this approach proved increasingly unsatisfactory. An attempt was made to work out a better solution, and to promulgate it as the orthodox one. But this could not be effectively done until Christianity became the religion of the Empire, and the Ecumenical Councils were held.

At Nicea (325) Athanasius was upheld as against Arius. Arius had taught that God created Jesus as his first creature, before anything else, and therefore Jesus was of a higher order than anything made subsequently. He had a human body, but not a genuine human nature; he was neither truly divine nor truly human. The Church could not tolerate this, and accepted Athanasius' formula that Jesus was "begotten" of the Father, not "made"; he was *not* the Father, but *homo ousios*, "of the same substance" with the Father.

The Council of Constantinople (381) acted to preserve not the true *deity* of Jesus, but his *humanity*. Apollinarius had maintained that in Christ the Divine Logos took the place of a human soul. This did not satisfy the Church. Jesus, it was believed, was a *true* man; he was *also* divine. He possessed *two natures* (one divine and one human) in *one person*. This was affirmed explicitly at Chalcedon (451). The Monophysites had been rebelling at this type of concept, and held to a *one-nature* theory, Jesus' person consisting for them, of a perfect blending of the human and the divine. They split off from the Great Church. The Third Council of Constantinople (681) ruled out the Monothelite heresy: the doctrine that Jesus had no human will apart from the Divine Will, a doctrine which denied the reality of Jesus' struggle against temptation, and made meaningless the recorded resolution of his conflict in Gethsemane when he prayed, "Not my will, but Thine, be done."

In Matthew 28:19, we read the words which Jesus is reported to have spoken to his followers after the resurrection: "Go ye therefore, and teach all nations, baptizing them in the name of the Father, and of the Son, and of the Holy Ghost." Most scholars admit that this formula is late, yet from the very beginning Christians had spoken of the Holy Spirit. Many regarded the Spirit either as a *mode* of God's action (as was the common Old Testament interpretation), or as a kind of agent subordinate to God. In either case the concept of God at the time was "binitarian" not "trinitarian." Even though the word *Trinitas* (*Trias* in Greek) came into use in the third century, referring to the threefold nature of the baptismal formula, this did *not* mean that people believed in the Holy Spirit as a *Person,* co-equal with the Father and the Son. It was obviously desirable for some ecumenical pronouncement to be made on the subject; so at the First Council of Constantinople (381) it was affirmed that the Spirit *was* a person (*hypostasis* in Greek) equal with the Father *and the* Son, "proceeding from" the Father; and this is the orthodox Catholic doctrine of the Trinity to this day. To the extent that a man is conceived as genuinely guided by the Holy Spirit, he is guided by one person of the Trinity. It is obvious that this view was accepted as generally as it was because of the strong Platonic tone of the prevailing philosophy.

All attempts to work out the implications of Christianity in terms of a monistic metaphysic failed to secure support. For instance, much earlier, the view of Sabellius that God was one and indivisible, with only one *hypostasis* but with three modes of operation, manifested in *succession,* was unsatisfactory to the Church. To some this view seemed plausible, and solved the problem by being monotheistic and trinitarian at the same time; God as Father existed until the birth of Christ; God was the Son while Jesus was on earth; God has been the Spirit since the resurrection. It was something like a man acting three parts, or performing three functions, one after the other. This notion is easily exploded by asking the question: Whom did Jesus pray to while on earth? Nevertheless, as Augustine felt strongly, Christian thinking often ran the risk of *tritheism:* the belief in three *separate* Gods. The Cappadocians, for example, hinted that God was "*impersonal* substance *personalized* as Father, Son and Spirit."[19] Augustine saw the danger here. He did not want the Church to be anything but monotheistic; so he wrote of God as one person who manifests himself in three ways; he compared the *persons* of the Trinity to memory, understanding, and will, or to memory, understanding, and love. He would have nothing to do with Gregory of Nyssa's analogy that Father, Son and Spirit are like Peter, James and John; this was to him tritheism. Augustine conceived of communion and prayer as not with any *one* person of the Trinity, but with one God, who was conceived as strongly personal. Though God's action in human life might be described as due to the Spirit-function, it is God who guides.

Augustine believed that God had created the universe out of nothing, and that it would tend to lapse away into nothingness unless sustained by his continuous activity. One aspect of this tendency to lapse is what we call the evil in the world. The cause of evil is not something positive. God allows evil partly because of his desire for variety, partly for the sake of a larger good. Sin in man shows itself in his tendency to choose the lesser rather than the greater good, to choose self rather than God. God guides men, if they will let him, into fellowship with himself. Man cannot choose aright without divine help. Everything that helps a man comes from God. All guidance, whether direct or indirect, is to be thought of in terms of a living God who wants men to have fellowship with him. In Augustine's thought, God permits evil that good may come; and if we cannot see the good, it is because of our limited vision and perspective.

We cannot know for sure, according to Augustine, whether or not we are saved; we could only know this by a *special* act of divine illumination. Freedom means freedom from evil, not freedom from restraint, and not genuine metaphysical freedom, at that. Actually, what we do is predestined, but God alone knows the details and can foresee the future. As far as salvation goes, Augustine thought of it as a future and not a present reality, but he also maintained that in this life the Christian may have a *glimpse* of that vision of God which will be his steady portion after death. Augustine's whole view of life is theocentric, and therefore Christ is chiefly significant as the greatest historical demonstration of the grace of God.

Augustine had no use for the distinction between natural and supernatural. Miracles, for him, needed no special explanation. He would not have worried over subtle differentiations between direct and indirect guidance. God was all in all, and could make his will known any way he chose. God worked through the regular forces of nature as well as independently of them, and one method of operation was no more or less divine than the other.

Augustine could never conceive of man as being able to save himself by rightly directing his own will, although Pelagius, his chief opponent, thought that was the correct way to look at the matter. Pelagius taught that God endowed man with free will, and with the gifts of reason and conscience. At first these natural gifts seemed sufficient, but the development of evil habits and attitudes and the influence of bad example made it necessary for God to vouchsafe additional divine revelation, which he did in the Law and then in the Gospel. More light still is given to those who use aright what they have.

There are many attractive features in Pelagius' view. He was supremely interested in the moral life of man. Although his belief in the possibility of Christian perfection made him many enemies, his emphasis on the reality of free will was accepted by many later theologians. However, the Church rejected him and his views. The Second Council of Orange (529) committed itself to a rather strongly Augustinian position, which A. C. McGiffert summed up in an epigram: "When men do evil they do their own will, when good the will of God." Thomas Aquinas attempted to combine whatever there was of worth in the moral attitude of Pelagius with the far more deeply religious view of Augustine, and Catholic theology today is the beneficiary of that remarkable synthesis.

With the coming of the thirteenth century a new period in the thinking of the western world begins, largely due to the rediscovery of Aristotle, whose writings had been the main inspiration of Averroes and the Arabian philosophical movement. Arabic translations of Aristotle's writings, with Averroean commentaries, also in Arabic, were brought to Europe and translated into Latin. Some teachers, upon the rediscovery of the great Greek thinker, experienced a new surge of intellectual vitality, and espoused his ideas vigorously. They were known as Averroists. The majority of Christian prelates were hostile. There were, however, some who adopted neither of these attitudes, but were simply anxious to learn what Aristotle had to say, and to incorporate the most reasonable features of his philosophy into the Christian system. Among these were Albertus Magnus and his pupil, Thomas Aquinas. They were convinced that

Aristotelianism had come to stay, and were as eager that Christianity should benefit from it as was Origen in his day that Christianity should benefit from Neo-platonism.

The writings of Thomas Aquinas form the basis of the Roman Catholic teaching. He recognized that Neo-platonic conceptions have been interwoven at almost every point with the inherited Jewish traditions and the historic doctrines of the Church; but he felt that Aristotle should also be reckoned with. He started from that great philosopher's notion that sense-experience is the source of all human knowledge. On the basis of this he felt that he could erect a "natural theology," embodying a belief in God as the great First Cause, a being who transcends time, possesses understanding, has a will, and wills the good. What he wills is not to be thought of as good because he arbitrarily wills it; but he wills it because it is good. Aquinas accepted Augustine's idea that God created the world out of nothing, but he felt that all things were created at once and do not have to be continually supported and renewed. Creation was not necessary to God, but was an act of free will, prompted by benevolence and directed by wisdom. Thomas believed that all these conclusions were the result of "natural" reasoning on the basis of sense experience and hence were consistently Aristotelian.

He did not conceive of man as a soul *inhabiting* a body, but as both soul and body; nevertheless, he believed strongly in personal immortality, and supported his belief by much subtle and elaborate reasoning. The average man can only know things by means of sense experience; therefore, he can have no direct revelation of God. But Aquinas believed that, in addition to the natural theology a man might work out for himself, there had come to prophets and apostles directly a *revealed* knowledge of God. When the average man is presented with this revealed theology through the Scriptures he realizes its truth because the Holy Spirit brings it home to him. Even prophets and apostles, with the exception of Moses and Paul, did not *see* the divine essence; their revelation was mediated to them by angels. But this revelation is a foretaste of the vision they are to enjoy beyond death; and the average man can live in the assurance that he also will have a vision of God after death, if he is saved.

Thomas conceived of God as acting through secondary causes. Thus the guidance for daily life received by the average Christian would be thought of as coming to him indirectly, through tradition, the Church, and through his own reason and conscience illumined by the truths of revealed religion. The Church is the great teacher both of right ideas and right behavior. A man should first of all possess the three so-called "theological" virtues: faith, hope, and charity; then come the four cardinal virtues: prudence, justice, fortitude, and temperance. He also mentioned as desirable Aristotle's tenfold classification: fortitude, temperance, liberality, magnificence, magnanimity, love of honor, clemency, friendship, truthfulness, and urbanity. Anyone who was able to embody this formidable catalogue of traits in his person would probably sprout wings and fly away.

Aquinas believed that the sacrifice of Christ shows us how much God loves us; it furnishes us the best example in history of utter obedience and humility; it frees us from sin and wins for us grace and glory. He held that the Holy Spirit is truly God, that love proceeds from him, and that he reveals to men their duties. Thomas was evidently not of a mystical temperament himself, but he allowed for a type of mysticism in his system by showing how choice souls can attain a *visio dei.*

There have been some extreme mystics in the Catholic tradition, such as Dionysius, who believed that the worshipper could become *substantially* a part of God in moments of ecstatic absorption. Others have claimed to have beatific visions, even though these were not thought of as communicable in language. But there have been still others, like Bernard of Clairvaux, who claimed only a constant desire to love God and do his will. Bernard was one of the first to emphasize the necessity for the imitation of the actual deeds and spirit of Christ. The characteristics which he particularly selected for emulation were humility and love; and this imitation of Jesus, which Bernard preached so convincingly, was lived out dramatically by another practical mystic, Francis of Assisi. It seems as if Christianity had so long been absorbed in theological speculation, thinking of the Divine Logos, and the relation of Christ to the Father and the Spirit, that it had lost sight of the man Jesus. And yet Jesus should surely be not only "the author and finisher of our faith" but our example as well; and from the time of Bernard and Francis onward there have been those for whom the chief appeal of Christianity is the figure of One who went about doing good, and who revealed God as wishing us to do likewise.

And so we see man using his creative imagination to form some adequate conception of God's image which will satisfy his deepest cravings for order and meaning in the universe, and for reality and richness in his devotional life. There are fragments of primitive animism forming part of the mosaic of our Jewish-Christian tradition, hints of superstitious belief in magic and divination, evidences of primitive polytheism, then of henotheism (where one God is worshipped but others are believed to exist) and monolatry. There are found, as time goes on, those daring prophetic monotheistic intuitions, interpreted as the response of sensitive seers to the pressure of the divine self-disclosure. In the great stream of thought and life which we call our own, we finally come to the life of One who impressed his most intimate followers as their clearest vision of the nature of the Deity, and the valiant but sometimes far-fetched attempts of Christian thinkers to express the inexpressible in terms of a Trinity of Divine Persons. The inadequacy of language to do justice to experience is everywhere apparent. Special terms are employed to describe what is essentially spaceless. The bitter arguments about whether the Spirit *proceeds* from the Father *and* the Son or only from the Father seem extraordinarily futile to us today. Let us face it: many of the thinkers who wrestled with the problems of theological definition were second or third rate. And yet every now and then we have a first-class man like Augustine writing things which are still worth reading, and not just setting down ideas which are studied today only as historically interesting curiosities.

Some moderns become so impatient with creed-makers that they deny the need for creeds at all; but this is an attitude which could never have seemed reasonable to a responsible Christian until long after the Reformation. Even those who decry the systematic definition of doctrine are often unacknowledged theologians in what they say or do *not* say about divine things. Even if we recognize the symbolic character of all religious language, we cannot help trying to find answers to ultimate questions; and if we try to state these answers, we straightway become theologians.

CHAPTER 5

The God of the Godly

It has often been said, a little too glibly, that the Protestant reformers merely substituted the authority of the Bible for the authority of the Church, and there is a real sense in which this is true. But Luther himself approached the problem from a different angle. In the last analysis, Luther's ultimate authority was the inner testimony of his own heart to the new life in Christ, to the freedom from fear which it brought, and to the vitality which accompanied the immortal hope of the free Christian soul. His own experience, he said, testified to the truth of the Gospel. The Gospel was found in the Bible; the Bible *contained* the word of God. The word of God was *not* identical with the Bible; some parts of Scripture were more helpful than others: the New Testament was superior to the Old; the Fourth Gospel, certain of Paul's letters, and I Peter, were superior to the rest of the New Testament; James was regarded as "an epistle of straw," and Revelation was worthless. His attitude towards Holy Writ was, therefore, far freer than that of his younger contemporary Calvin, or of the present-day Fundamentalists. Yet in spite of this, it is true that in the Leipzig Colloquy of 1519 he appealed *from* the Church *to* the Bible. It was impressed upon him that some recognized authority was needed on which man could depend, apart from his own direct religious experience; and this authority was the Word of God as found in the Bible, to be appropriated by devout reading, and by complete surrender to Christ. The Holy Spirit quickened the hearts of those who steeped themselves in the Word, and thus gave them guidance in matters of faith and conduct.

Calvin agreed with Luther on this particular issue. He wrote:

"I simply confess what is the truth, that the Lord is continually helping those who are his and guiding them with his Spirit. That this Spirit is not a Spirit of error, of ignorance, of falsehood or of darkness; but a Spirit of sure revelation, wisdom and light, from which they may infallibly learn what is bestowed on them, that is: what is the hope of their calling and what the riches of the glory of the inheritance of God in the Saints." [1]

Men can get only a foretaste of the Spirit while they are in the flesh, and therefore the safest guide for daily life is the use of one's understanding in interpreting and applying the Scriptures. Calvin was here aiming a barb at the Roman Church as a source of "external leadership," but he was equally concerned about those licentious people who claimed to be "guided" spiritually, even in their moral aberrations. He believed that no one should boast about being in possession of the Spirit, nor should anyone conceive of himself as guided by the Spirit *apart from* the Word.

Of course, Calvin's attitude towards the Scripture was different from that of Luther, in that he believed in the equal inspiration of *all* parts of the Bible; thus one finds in him, and in a long procession of Protestant thinkers, a minimizing of the "enthusiastic" and mystical aspects of

Christianity, and a stressing of absolute obedience to the will of God as revealed in the Old and New Testaments.

The concept of God against which the Reformers rebelled was that of a Mighty Sovereign, ruling over a vast hierarchical system, sanctioning an elaborate apparatus for the forgiveness of sin. Confession, absolution, penance, indulgence—all these were considered necessary to salvation by the Church. God, therefore, although still theoretically available to the believer as a direct source of comfort, was actually conceived as requiring all sorts of deeds and "works" before assurance of salvation could be vouchsafed. To make matters worse, the indulgences which the Holy Father was commissioned to grant *freely* were now being *sold,* and had become one of the chief sources of the Church's support. Only by the most devious reasoning could any sanction for this be found in the Bible, but from the standpoint of the institution, it was not necessary to find definite Biblical sanction for ecclesiastical practices; God had empowered the councils of the Church to declare his will and to decide how man should fulfill it.

Luther had been all through the struggle to achieve the inner assurance of salvation by doing "good works," by subjecting himself to rigid discipline, by following courses of austere—almost masochistic—privation. He never found what he was looking for, until the day when the verse, "The just shall live by faith," leaped out at him from the Epistle to the Romans. That statement struck him with the force of a new revelation. From then on he thought of God as dealing directly with him, in terms of "faith" and not of "works." The burden was lifted from his heart; much of the worry disappeared from his mind. He lived in the assurance of God's acceptance; but he was not always sure of himself; never was he cocksure. From time to time he still questioned the validity of his complete shift of emphasis; at one point he asked himself: "How often has my trembling heart palpitated—are you alone the wise one? Are all the others in error?"

But he was not alone for long, nor had he really been "alone" before. Luther's rediscovery of Paul, and of the early Church's direct personal experience of God in Christ, whether thought of as the work of "The Father" or "The Lord" or "The Spirit," had been the mainstay of many pious hearts throughout the Middle Ages, and was now to be the basis for the new departures. God was again very near, very personal, very intimate, for all his grandeur and austerity. And among the duties the Reformers felt he laid on them was the challenging of the entire institutional system, a system which the Pope claimed to be the earthly embodiment of the heavenly will. Nowhere in Christian history is the contrast in divine images sharper than at this point, for all the creedal similarity between what both Catholics and Protestants conceived to be God's attributes and "mighty works." It makes a tremendous difference whether or not one feels that the chances of securing God's attention and enlisting his sympathy are increased by the intercession of the Virgin, the saints, heavenly beings and the like. It makes a tremendous difference whether or not God's grace is thought of as freely given without intermediaries.

Most human beings who have a convincing experience of God's presence and salvation and acceptance are inclined to conclude that their creedal and ethical judgments are also his. There may seem to be no sure way of distinguishing between a projected and a revealed concept of God, or a projected and revealed interpretation of the Divine Will. The Roman Church can fall back on the decisions of the councils and the pronouncements of the pontiffs to decide what is divinely sanctioned; but this will not satisfy the non-Roman Christian. Those who believe in the Word of God as the final authority can fall back on the Bible, if what the Bible says is unambiguous on any given point; but this may not convince one who approaches Scripture as a Christian "liberal." Furthermore, circumstances change, and the Bible itself gives evidence of a development in both theology and morals which makes it almost impossible to employ as an unequivocal guide. The Reformers understood this problem, but for some of them the only solution seemed to be to set up new orthodoxies in place of Rome's and declare those who disagreed with them heretics. Thus the followers of Luther and Zwingli separated on the interpretation of the Lord's Supper. Erasmus, "reformer" though he was, repudiated Luther and refused to break with Rome. Calvin set up an authoritarian regime in Geneva, and worked for Servetus' execution. And sect after sect was founded upon some new version of an old doctrine.

A place where one might suspect that Luther's human convictions affected his interpretation of the Divine Will was in his attitude towards the Peasants' War. It is possible to argue that God's view of all wild, unbridled, cruel and destructive rebellion is one of disapproval, but it is difficult to see his Holy Spirit evidenced in tracts like Luther's "Against the Murdering, Thieving Hordes of Peasants." Luther wrote, "Let every one who can smite, slay and stab, secretly or openly, remembering that nothing can be more poisonous, hurtful or devilish than a rebel. It is just as when one must kill a mad dog; if you don't strike him he will strike you, and the whole land with you."

Dr. Fosdick labels this an "outrageous tract" which "left an indelible stain on Luther's reputation, and the Peasants' War itself, in which the rebels were mercilessly exterminated, put the fear of revolution—by many identified with the Reformation—into the minds of German rulers. The cause of religious reform was seriously injured, and in Luther's thinking a deep distrust of the common people was engendered which affected him throughout his life, and made Lutheranism for many years inimical to democracy in church and state."[2] One can easily see why Luther felt the way he did; a modern Protestant has difficulty in believing that God was solidly behind such an intemperate attitude. Possibly Wesley's definition of a Methodist as one who " 'does good unto all men,' unto neighbors and strangers, friends and enemies" captures better what many of our contemporaries would call the authentic accent of the New Testament.

Moving to a slightly later period, it is not difficult to understand why Calvin felt it necessary to rule Geneva the way he did. He was fighting what E. H. Harbison calls a "two-front war of ideas from the very beginning against Romanism on the right and Anabaptism on the left."[3] Luther was up against the same dual struggle. Neither could tolerate religion without order and authority; they rejected Catholic authority as presumptuously unscriptural, but they rejected radical voluntarism as dangerously revolutionary.

Calvin's concept of God was not original with him, but the emphasis he placed on one of God's attributes—absolute sovereignty—was. Luther's belief that in salvation "God does everything, man nothing,"[4] easily opened the way for the Genevan reformer's insistence on the divine omnipotence and omniscience. God "has once and for all determined, both whom he would admit to salvation, and whom he would condemn to destruction."[5] "If he willed to ruin all mankind, he has the right to do it, and in those whom he rescues from perdition one can contemplate nothing but his sovereign goodness. We acknowledge, therefore, the elect to be the recipients of his mercy (as they truly are) and the rejected to be recipients of his wrath, a wrath, however, which is nothing but just." [6] This may not appear just by human standards; but God does not will something because it is just by human standards; it is just "because he wills it." [7]

Many modern Christians find this aspect of Calvin's theology uncongenial to their way of thinking. The image of God in the *Institutes* and the *Instruction* seems out of harmony with that suggested by the parables of the lost sheep, the lost coin and the lost son in Luke 15. On the other hand, there are passages in the Synoptics which, with a slight change of emphasis, can be interpreted as reinforcing the propriety of Calvin's concept. In Matthew 25 the "unprofitable servant" knows that his master is a "hard man," is accused of being "wicked and slothful," is cast into "outer darkness" where there is "weeping and gnashing of teeth." Again, the "Son of man," who has "come in his glory," says to "them on the left hand, Depart from me, ye cursed, into everlasting fire, prepared for the devil and his angels." No matter how figurative and symbolic these passages may be, they still give us, as we saw in Chapter 3, a glimpse of divine wrath, sternness, judgment. The one element which Calvin highlights and which the New Testament omits or soft-pedals is any suggestion of *arbitrariness* in God. In Matthew 25, the servant is pictured as having been negligent and derelict; the "goats" had refused to minister to "one of these least." The punishment meted out was for a failure to perform a duty. Those who set forth the Synoptic teaching, in the form in which we have it, were quite clear that God had given all men a chance to do his will, to express love for others, to show compassion, and that some failed to embrace that opportunity. Nothing is said or implied about the taint of original sin. Nothing is said or implied about some being elected to do God's will and others rejected; nothing is hinted about any foregone conclusion that certain people will be "saved" and certain others "damned." The Synoptic emphasis seems to be on God's giving everyone a chance, involving freedom to obey or to disobey. It is, therefore, at this point that the theology of the Gospels seems somewhat different from the theology of Geneva.

However, indications of the predestinarian concept are to be found in Paul, and in the stream of thought and life that flows from Paul through Augustine and Luther to Calvin. It is, again, a matter of emphasis. Calvin was a logician. He was a systematic thinker where Luther was not. His *Institutes* occupy relatively the same position in Reformation thought that Aquinas' *Summa* occupies in Catholic thought. After suffering something of an eclipse in the 1920s, Calvin is again being studied and analyzed.

Calvin was a strict disciplinarian, as he conceived his God to be. He felt that the only way to bring moral order out of the chaos of Geneva was to give the community a rigid regime. He condemned a man to prison for smiling during a baptismal service. He jailed another for sleeping during a sermon. He imprisoned others for playing games, for gambling on the result of a game, for breaking the Sabbath. He sanctioned banishment and capital punishment for heretics.[8]

He carried the logic of his position to its frightening conclusion. When commenting on an Old Testament account of God's sanctioning the destruction of Sihor's cities, including the men, women and children, Calvin wrote:

"We may rest assured that God would suffer only those infants to be destroyed whom he had already damned and destined to eternal death." [9] And yet he believed in the mercy of God, the self-giving of the Father in sending his Son, and the compassion of the Divine Grace. We are here confronted with a complex character, with a subtly complex theology, propounded in a turbulent age to men who, while needing assurance of the love of God also needed a stern reminder of God's judgment.

At the opposite end of the scale from Rome, the radical Protestant sects—Anabaptists and others—conceived of God as directly available to the worshipper without any intermediaries, and as concerned chiefly with a "gathered" company of saints, who were perforce "in" the world but were certainly not "of" it. God was thought of as trusting these groups of believers to elect their own pastors and regulate their own religious life. The end of the age was felt to be at hand. This conviction was sometimes linked with the belief that the "separatists" were to be agents of God to bring about the downfall of the old order. Sometimes it eventuated in pietism and quietism. In either case, the image of God held by the sects was very different from that of Rome; this difference still exists, is now more clearly defined than ever, and helps to account for the great gap which separates the Protestant left wing, not only from Rome, but from those denominations which believe in a measure of ecclesiastical and creedal discipline.

It will not serve our purpose to enter into a detailed discussion of the nuances and refinements of divine concepts which resulted from the fragmentation of Christianity following the Reformation; but it may be instructive to examine the ideas of a few leaders, each of whom represents an important approach to the problems: how shall we conceive of God? And, what is his will for us? We shall consider briefly George Fox, John Wesley, the Seventh Earl of Shaftesbury, and David Livingstone.

George Fox, in seventeenth-century England, started a movement which has had a tremendous effect, even outside of the circle of Friends, on the whole idea of the character of God and the nature of his operation. Fox, at an early age, was thought of as possessing a different temperament from the majority of men—"More religious, inward, still, solid and observing" as one biographer writes. He was apprenticed to a shoemaker until he was nineteen, and gained the reputation of being a fine, pure, upstanding, and honest lad. He came to be tremendously impressed with the wickedness and frivolity of the world and he felt called upon to do something about it. He tells us that "at the command of God," on July 9, 1643, he left home and wandered about, "trying to find some effective message and purpose." One day, he says, "the Lord opened to him" that the true believers had to be born again. After this, he had frequent deep mystical experiences, in which the sense of direct divine communication became increasingly stronger. In his *Journal* we read of a constantly recurring series of "leadings" and "drawings" and "openings." George Fox never minimized the direction one might receive from the Scriptures, but he insisted that its guidance was only available to those who were "in the same spirit as that in which the Scriptures were given forth."

In 1649, he was admonished by an inner voice to enter a church (which he called a "steeple house") and protest against the cold, legalistic, secondhand, doctrinal type of religion there preached. From that day on, he urged people to give themselves over to the guidance of God in Christ. His intense belief in this, and his outspoken denunciation of those who disagreed with him, led him to prison for blasphemy over and over again. In some ways, he was ethically sensitive to a remarkable degree; in other ways, he condemned puritanically many harmless customs and amusements. At times, his complete confidence in the reliability of his own guidance was indistinguishable from plain stubbornness. But with all his faults and extremes, he was a man of penetrating religious insight, and the movement which began with him has been a steadily vitalizing factor in the world ever since. The late Rufus M. Jones, surely one of the most winsome of twentieth-century philosophers and teachers, has done a great deal to express in telling language the religious values of Quakerism, the chief of which are its profound concern about real mystical experience as the birthright of every Christian, and its steady emphasis on the fruits of that mysticism in a life of simplicity, dignity, and ethical sensitivity.

God is conceived as an intensely personal, omnipresent being, immanent in all things as well as transcendent, readily available to each faithful person as a source of light and leading. No intermediary of any kind is required. No sacrament, priest, creed, or institution stands in any interpretive or authoritative relationship to the humble believer as more important to his religious life than the illumination he receives directly in simple, mystical communion. All anyone needs to do is to open his heart to God, turn his attention towards the Divine, sincerely desire to know the Father's will. Guidance and strength will be given immediately in the form of promptings, leadings and "concerns." The practical mysticism of the Friends takes seriously Paul's injunction to "pray without ceasing." Almost all other

Christian groups officially recognize the immediate availability of the Spirit, but no other fellowship stresses as constantly the primacy of the individual's intimate, personal *rapport* with God as finally normative.

It was John Wesley's association with a small company of Moravian Pietists in London in 1738 which gave him the fresh religious impulse which he needed so badly. He had, for many years before this, been an ordained minister of unusual piety, but he always afterwards referred to his experience of that year as his "conversion." He wrote, in describing it: "I felt my heart strangely warmed, I felt I did trust in Christ, and an assurance was given to me that he had taken away my sins, even mine, and saved me from the law of sin and death." [10] Even after this he placed his emphasis on the experience of the individual Christian as the important test of religion, and on the Reformation doctrine of salvation by faith alone, issuing in but not dependent on works. Wesley and the evangelicals after him declared that "all men are born in sin and shapen in wickedness"; thus the atoning work of Christ was necessary, and regeneration crucial. In common with Augustine, man was conceived as not being able to do God's will in his own strength. Not only was the Holy Spirit necessary to help a man turn to God but also to continue to live as he should. Christian perfection, meaning the "uninterrupted reign of love in the heart," was attainable by the surrendered man, the Spirit acting upon the converted person with a steady supernatural influence.[11]

The moral life of which God approves and which therefore is dictated by the Spirit was thought to be puritanical and other-worldly. It would lead a man to give up such things as card-playing, dancing, gambling, horse-racing, theatre-going, drinking, costly dressing and adornment, and frivolity of all kinds. But along with this went a zeal for practical service. God was conceived as desiring man not only to keep himself "unspotted from the world," but also to engage in acts of mercy and charity. The moral life was not one of merely doing one's duty, of coldly and systematically applying to daily living the injunctions of the Spirit and the precepts of the Bible. The life of religion should be one of warmth and feeling.

The operation of the Holy Spirit in the believer's heart enabled him to distinguish right from wrong, truth from falsehood. Faith was not felt to rest upon argument or apologetic, but upon direct vision given by God. The Spirit could reveal his will through the Scriptures, even when appealed to at random in times of indecision, as in the case of Tennyson's "Enoch Arden." And thus we find, in the literature of historic Methodism, that emphasis upon the direct availability of God for the converted life, which involves the view that the Deity is an active personal agent, with strict moral standards and an evangelistic purpose, ready to use the surrendered individual for the saving of others.

God has not always been thought of as interested in what have come to be called social questions. Within evangelical denominations we find a wide spectrum of opinion, ranging from reaction to radicalism. The attitude of some Christians towards wealth and poverty has been neatly expressed in a stanza of a hymn, now fortunately forgotten by most people:

> The rich man in his castle,
> The poor man at the gate,
> God made them high or lowly
> And ordered their estate.

One does not have to be a socialist to resent this picture of a God who deliberately created social classes. All down through Christian history there have been those who emphasized the loving-kindness of God and his solicitude towards those deprived of opportunity by conditions over which they had no control. And so we have had John Howard believing that God abominated the conditions which had been allowed to prevail in the prisons of England. We have had William Wilberforce believing that God abominated the traffic in human slaves. And we have had Anthony Ashley Cooper, the Seventh Earl of Shaftesbury, believing that God abominated the conditions under which men, women and children had to work in nineteenth-century British factories, mills, and mines.

In the second quarter of that century in England, there was no age requirement for employment. Boys and girls of five, six and seven, if they worked at all, were required to be on the job in many machine shops twenty out of the twenty-four hours, sometimes never going home at all, but collapsing on the straw under the machines for whatever sleep they got. The children below ground in the mines were harnessed like dogs to coal-carts, which they dragged from pit to lift in the dusty darkness. Others stood for twelve hours on end, ankle-deep in water, working the pumps. Youngsters known as "climbing boys" were virtually the slaves of men who forced them to clean chimneys from the inside while their masters kept them at work and collected the fees. The conditions among victims of mental illness were incredible. The afflicted were imprisoned in cells, bound with chains, lashed by brutal guards for obstreperousness, and exhibited to curiosity-seekers for their fascination or amusement. The slums of some of our cities today are noisome enough, but the slums of London one hundred years ago would be quite unendurable to a modern visitor. A man of noble birth like Shaftesbury would not normally have had to see much of all this. The aristocrats were often completely isolated from any contact with the destitute and miserable. It was by chance that young Anthony Cooper, as a schoolboy, witnessed the spectacle which changed the direction of his thought and life.

While at Harrow, he happened to pass a churchyard where a poor man was being unceremoniously buried. Those handling the rude casket let it slip; it fell to the ground, burst open, and exposed to young Anthony's horrified gaze the pathetic, emaciated body. The question the lad put to himself was: "Can this happen simply because a man is poor and without friends?" Later he said that, during the fifteen minutes following the shock of this experience, he decided upon his career: He would work to relieve the sufferings and humiliations of the unfortunate. A tablet on a wall there may be seen to this day, carrying the inscription:

"Near this spot Anthony Ashley Cooper, afterwards the Seventh Earl of Shaftesbury, K.G., while yet a boy in Harrow School saw with Shame and Indignation the Pauper's Funeral which helped to awaken his lifelong Devotion to the Service of the Poor and Oppressed."

At the age of twenty-five he entered Parliament, was appointed to several important posts and seemed to have a brilliant future ahead of him. But two years later he had his chance to implement his boyhood concern: he was made a member of a commission to inquire into the treatment of "lunatics." He visited the asylums himself and brought back such hair-raising tales to Parliament that he started the process which finally resulted in a complete reform of the Lunacy Acts. In his forties he secured the passage of a law forbidding the employment of women in mines, and of children under thirteen; later he pushed through a ten-hour-a-day working law against the stubborn opposition of many ostensibly devout Christians in the government and out. He organized schools for under-privileged children; he sponsored the Lodging House Act, which Charles Dickens called "the best piece of legislation that ever proceeded from the English Parliament." In his seventies, he successfully sponsored the Chimney-Sweeps Bill which ended the danger and injustice of the old "climbing-boys" system. At one point in his life he quelled a riot of the poor against the rich; and at their own suggestion he met, like a modern Ali Baba but animated by a different purpose, with forty thieves for some of whom he secured the opportunity to start life all over again in Australia. Martin Davidson writes, "Lord Shaftesbury had great faults. He is said to have had no tact, he was conservative and aristocratic by nature, and he was no popular leader. Nor was he far ahead of his time; most of his achievements were cures of existing social disorders; he worked *for* the oppressed rather than *with* them. He was strongly opposed to labor unions; yet he was always regarded as their friend by the poor and the down-and-out." [12]

Constance Smith ends her study of Shaftesbury with these words: "He awakened the paralyzed public conscience of nineteenth-century England. But he did more than this. An awakened public conscience, if it is not to spend itself in futile emotion, must find a channel of expression. Shaftesbury taught it to speak with the voice of law, and the lesson which he gave to his own generation now resounds throughout the civilized world."

For our study, the important matter is Lord Shaftesbury's conception of God. He was a convinced Christian, and, as far as we know, shared the theology of the Church of England. He prayed earnestly before any important undertaking, was a regular attendant at worship, and gave generously of his time, energy, and money to the Y.M.C.A., the London City Mission, the movement for holding informal services in theatres and music halls, the British and Foreign Bible Society, and the missionary outreach of Christianity. It is obvious that he believed in a God who wanted men to organize their lives so that law was on the side of reasonable opportunity for all, and against the exploitation of the weak by the strong, the poor by the rich. In this Shaftesbury was typical of many Christians since his day, especially in our western tradition. These men and women are well aware that God took a desperate risk in giving men freedom, a freedom which can be used by some to gain dominion over others, but which can also be used to build a system which promotes the welfare of *all.* We now take it for granted that "an awakened public conscience" should "speak with the voice of law," and that God is always trying to persuade men of his concern that it should. Christians may differ violently on *how much* social control is necessary to achieve reasonable opportunity for everyone; but there is not much difference of opinion on the necessity for some, and by concentrating on the passage of humanitarian legislation during almost sixty years of public life, the Seventh Earl of Shaftesbury demonstrated to the world his faith in a God who cares for *all* his children, and who has revealed himself supremely in One who "went about doing good."

Lord Shaftesbury believed in missions, but he never became a foreign missionary himself. He had other work to do at home, in Parliament, in England; but his financial support followed his concern for the bringing of the Gospel to India, China, Africa and elsewhere. Without the Shaftesburys there could not have been the Livingstones, who are convinced that God has a special commission for some to take the message of Christ to those who have never heard it.

I served in the foreign field for several years, and I am well aware of all the criticisms of missionary work which have been leveled against it by both the informed and the uninformed. I have seen extraordinarily narrow-minded evangelists proclaiming with great fervor and sincerity the existence of a God who seems like a caricature of the Father of our Lord Jesus Christ. One day in language-school I sat next to a newly arrived Christian worker who was reading a denominational magazine. The class had not begun, and as I evinced an interest in the journal he was perusing, he let me look at it. On the front page was a picture of a handsome African native in a long white robe, and under the photograph I read: "The first Anuak in heaven." I was fascinated to know how the editor was sure enough of this to write the caption. It seems that the man in the picture was the first convert among the Anuaks, that he had been baptized by a worker from the denomination publishing the magazine, but that he had been drowned soon after being received into the Church. I was puzzled about the cocksureness of the editor's use of the term "first," to say nothing of "heaven." The missionary countered my skepticism with, "Yes, I see what you mean. Some other Anuak might have been converted and baptized about whom we know nothing." I did not bother to tell him that was not what I meant!

Nevertheless, some people with what we might think are limited points of view have had very big hearts, and have been much better than their theology. Others, whose main motive has been evangelism, but who have also done effective educational, agricultural and medical work, have felt that God was with them as they engaged in *all* these pursuits. Missionary work at its best has been statesmanlike, sociologically sound, and helpful to peoples struggling to shake off the shackles of superstition, dependence, and ignorance. It has been western Christendom's answer to what the Early Church reported Jesus as saying to his followers after the resurrection, "Go ye into all the world, and preach the gospel to every creature."

I have known a missionary who believed that God did not want Christians to sing hymns but only metrical versions of the Psalms, and who tied up hundreds of dollars of mission funds in Psalm-books so that his successor would be under no temptation to purchase hymn-books! Yet I have also known a missionary who was such a broad-gauge human being that our government appointed him its ambassador to the country in which he had worked as a Christian educator.

In this connection one thinks of David Livingstone. The inscription on the slab of black marble in Westminster Abbey, where his body lies buried, reads:

"Brought by faithful hands over land and sea, here rests David Livingstone, Missionary, Traveler, Philanthropist, born Mar. 19, 1813, at Blantyre, Lanarkshire, (Scotland). Died May 4, 1873, at Chitambos' Village, Ilala, (Central Africa). For thirty years his life was spent in an unwearied effort to evangelize the native races, to explore the undiscovered secrets, and abolish the desolating slave trade of Central Africa, where, with his last words, he wrote, 'All I can say in my solitude is may Heaven's rich blessing come down on every one—American, English, Turk—who will help to heal the open sore of the world.'"

The world still has its "open sores," and will continue to have them, but those who have faith in the Christian God believe that he desires them to be *healers,* no matter where their mission of healing takes them, no matter what it costs them. It has been often said by humanitarians that the necessity for "healing" is apparent no matter whether one believes in God or not. This is, of course, true. But it is also true that one's idea of God affects his view of society, its progress and welfare. A belief as to what God desires may be a rationalization of the social values one cherishes, derived from human experience; but however a man comes by an idea of what God's will is, it will affect what he does, if he takes it seriously. If tribesmen in North India believe that Kali is pleased by the slaughter of white men, white men will be slaughtered with a relish all the more spicy because of its divine sanction. If Allah in the Koran is believed to have given his blessing to plural marriages, it will be very difficult to persuade Muslims that polygamy is wrong.

Once in the late twenties, my Egyptian students and I motored with a doctor to a little village in the Delta, where we tried to convince the people that they should not drink water from the irrigation-ditches but use their well-water instead. We showed them, in a microscope, the difference between the bacteria-laden ditch-water and the purer water from a private pump. The former was crawling with animulculae; the latter was almost completely clear. The doctor told them that the one would make them ill, possibly kill them, whereas the other would be beneficial. One of the Muslim teachers of the village stepped up to the microscope to have his look. He felt that he must show off his learning, since the *effendis* (modern young men) were exhibiting theirs, so he quoted from the *Koran:* "For every life there is a period written. It can neither be hurried up nor delayed." Then he expounded, "Therefore, O your Excellency the Doctor, it is all folly for you to say that these little animals can kill a man. If the man's time has come to die, he will die. If not, he will live."

The doctor replied, "O my brother, you are a wise man. Please tell me, what do you do when you are walking along a railroad track and hear the engine whistle? Do you continue walking on the track or get off?"

"It is well known," answered the *sheikh*, "that any intelligent man will get off the track or else he will be killed."

"You answer discreetly, O teacher," said the doctor, "for you do not believe that it is written in Paradise that you are to die by that engine, and so you do not defy it but wisely let it pass. Now, simply imagine that these microbes are like the engine, able to kill you if you do not keep out of their way; and, believing that your fate is not to die by them, you carefully avoid them."

The view that Allah determines everything that happens, that the unfolding of time is like the unrolling of an intricately woven rug whose pattern is already complete but cannot be known by man before it is unrolled—this has practical consequences which interfere with the proper teaching of science and the proper conduct of life. Sometimes the conception of Allah's activity involves a belief that he alone determines *from instant to instant* the events which, as we look back on them, are accepted as inevitable. In either case, any study of conditions which have to be fulfilled before the desired results will take place seems to be somewhat beside the point. Modern Islamic philosophers are trying to rethink their theology to allow for the practical freedom which the contemporary scientist must feel if he is to work experimentally. Modern Egypt finds that it has to proceed in many fields without trying to square its procedures with the *Koran*. Modern women do not care for the Koranic edict, "Men are in charge of women, because Allah hath made the one of them to excel the other," or its many parallel sentiments. One's view of God and what he wants is determinative for a religious person. A change in this view, if it impresses him as reasonable, will inevitably affect his way of life. Hence the importance which missionaries have always placed on the preaching of a Deity who requires a man that he "do justly," "love mercy," and "walk humbly" with his God, and that in the Christian fellowship "there is neither Jew nor Greek, there is neither bond nor free, there is neither male nor female." If Micah's prophecy and Paul's Epistle to the Galatians are taken in dead earnest, the view of God and his will for men are bound to effect an important transvaluation of values.

Livingstone was brought up in a home of simple faith and steady toil. Early in life he was impressed by the words of an old man of Blantyre, "Now lad, make religion the everyday business of your life, and not a thing of fits and starts." He worked hard at his books, even to the point of propping one up above the loom when he became a cotton-spinner. Later he went to school, began to study medicine in college, but he volunteered as a foreign missionary before he had finished his course. When the veteran Robert Moffat told him that "in Africa on a sunny morning" he might see "the smoke rising from a thousand villages where the name of Christ has never been heard," he knew where he wanted to go. He firmly believed that the example of white settlers whose relations with the native peoples were carried on in a truly Christian spirit would pave the way for the spread of the Gospel.

The story of his thirty-year struggle to explore the

country, to defeat the slave trade, to evangelize, to study the needs of the people, is well known. Dogged by weariness and ill health, crushed by the loss of his wife, depressed by the antagonism of tribes which were stirred up against him by the slave traders, he nevertheless continued to work for the cause he believed in. He felt the companionship of God in Christ whose commission he bore and whose faith he proclaimed. It is both significant and symbolic that when he died his heart was buried by his native friends under a tree in Ilala.

We have considered some of the mountain-peaks of Protestant faith and life in the work of men like Luther, Calvin, Fox, Wesley, Shaftesbury and Livingstone, with the idea that their views of God are supremely worth our attention. It is obvious that they have much in common. It is also obvious that each represents a different emphasis. The common elements come from a common devotion to the God of the Bible. The differences stem from diversities of temperament, background, education, and the historical situation faced by each. It is inevitable that God should be imagined, by any deeply committed person, as concerned about what that person feels to be the crying need of his age. A person's value-judgment as to what primarily needs to be done will be determined partly by objective considerations, and partly by his own temperament and emotional needs. One might imagine that Luther's personal experience affected his view of God's will more than did Shaftesbury's, but it is impossible to be dogmatic about a matter of this kind—impossible and unnecessary. Certainly each of the men we have considered was dominated by a devotion to an image of God derived from an important aspect of Biblical theology. Each one believed that God had an important task for him to perform. Each one was convinced that God was with him as his unseen companion and his divine support. Each felt that "of himself" he could "do nothing," but that "through Christ" he could be "more than conqueror."

CHAPTER 6

The God of the Guided

MOST contemporary Protestant thinkers conceive of God as one who holds *communion* with his children, but there is a difference of opinion among them on the subject of God's *communication.* Let us now examine, as typical of the thought of many who believe that God "speaks" to man, directly and unmistakably, the theory of divine guidance which was held by the members of the Oxford Group a few years ago, and is now held by those of the Moral Re-Armament Movement, its spiritual legatee. M.R.A. has no monopoly on the belief in, and the practice of, direct divine guidance, but it makes a very special point of it. The view of God implied in the theory adds something to what we have already set forth. God becomes an unseen Friend who directs the choices, guides the decisions, and manages the lives of those who put their trust in him and surrender their wills to his will. The ways in which God enters dynamically into human experience to stir the mind, to aid recollection, to reinforce the will, to warn, to comfort, and illumine cannot be explained, claim the apologists for this position, in terms of ordinary psychology. The Holy Spirit (used interchangeably with the term God) can help a person decide which of two courses of action is the right one with unmistakable clarity. Of course, this would be true for all Christians if the decision involved alternatives of right and wrong, or good and best, and where the conscious confrontation of the divine would serve to sensitize the conscience and reinforce the will. But those who believe in specific divine guidance go way beyond this, and testify to God's practical direction in matters where, superficially at least, the problem is not at all of clear-cut ethical values, but of selection among several perfectly good ways to proceed.

God's chief concern, according to the Moral Re-Armament Movement, is to bring peace and brotherhood to the world through the devotion of guided individuals. As Dr. Frank N. D. Buchman, its outstanding leader, expresses it: "When man listens, God gives him ideas. And when man chooses to be governed by these ideas, he becomes a new type of Man . . . The challenge of our times is simply this. Will the scientists, the statesmen, the men of the factory, school and farm, face the facts? Test them? Act on them and live accordingly? Ideas quick and powerful to reconcile nations, to conquer all hearts and wills, to inspire a world-wide renaissance, are instantly available, immediately applicable. For ideas are God's weapons for a new world. And every man, if he will, can listen to God."

The strategy of M.R.A. is on a much grander scale than was that of the Oxford group of twenty and thirty years ago. International and political problems now bedevil the world. The tension between East and West relaxes for a while only to become taut and dangerous again. But the basic principles of action remain the same: to persuade men and women to surrender their lives to God, and allow themselves to be guided by him in everything they do. A surrendered person will get direction as to whom to approach to win new converts to the movement. He must use his own mind to the best of his ability, but his knowledge is very limited, and he will need the wisdom of an omniscient Mind to enlighten him as to his most significant opportunities. When a chance to help someone is seized, God is active in directing the interview, helping the worker to be tactful and effective.

God is believed to have a plan for every life. God's plan for a man's existence fits in with the larger strategy of building that community of guided spirits which Christ called the Kingdom. Man is free to accept or reject the plan God has for him. His freedom is not only apparent and practical but real and metaphysical. God sees a great deal of what is going to happen in the future—and he often guides an individual on the basis of his foresight in matters which are, humanly speaking, absolutely beyond the possibility of human prevision, in order to make sure that the right man is in the right place at the right time to perform some helpful deed or to speak some redeeming word. God is not thought of as having complete foreknowledge. The analogy of the divine chess-player, set forth by William James, is suggestive at this point. God knows the results of all possible moves in his game with man. Man has a choice of moves, and it is a *real* choice. God does not always know *how* man will move; but as soon as any move is made, God can then foresee the results of the move as they affect the game.

But of course, God is *not* an antagonist or an opponent; possibly it would be better to think of him as watching our game with Life. We are, to a certain extent, possibly only to a limited extent, free agents—but we *are* free to move. God knows the results of every possible move we may make, but he does not know every move we *will* make. The freedom that he has given us is real, and is based upon a definite self-limitation of his knowledge and power. He wants to help us win the game, if we will let him. He will guide us as to the next move, if we will permit him, by surrendering ourselves to his will. He does not wish us to appeal to him if a move could obviously be made on the basis of common sense alone. But we are making disastrous moves, due to wilfulness and ignorance and a false sense of our own treasured independence of all counsel except that of our own puny minds. At any given moment, he has a plan for us, which would involve making a certain move, with certain results. If, however, we miss the plan and make a false move, he then has a second move to suggest, if we will listen. If we again make a false move, he has a third, the result of which may not be as good as if we had followed his guidance two moves back, but still this later plan of campaign will redeem as much of the game as is left.

Analogies such as this are, of course, crude and in many ways misleading. In a game it would be considered unethical to get guidance from a third person to win, no matter who that person might be. But life is not a game; and no one doubts the right of anyone to get whatever help he can in solving his problems. Supernatural help should be very welcome indeed.

The author of a widely read pamphlet on guidance says: "Those cautious people who speak of the 'dangers of young people trying to be guided' need only be introduced to the problems one meets daily in the lives of all kinds of people to know the terrible dangers of *not* being guided. The tragic problem of the 'misfit' is one. There are no misfits in God's plan. The tragedy is when God's plan is missed. That he can provide a second or third plan does not lessen our responsibility to see that those with their lives before them do not miss the glory of fulfilling God's purpose."

Not all thoughts are guidance, even for a "guided" person. Of course, there are many completely or almost completely "unguided" people, who have deliberately cut themselves off from the voice of the Spirit by sin, whose purposes apparently fit in at no point with the cause of God in the world. Even here, however, the Spirit can trouble what is left of the conscience, through another person's example or testimony, or directly, or both. But even in the case of the saints, purely human desires and promptings besiege them at times, and are occasionally mistaken for whisperings of the Divine. In routine matters divine direction is often unnecessary. One normally would not try to be "guided" as to what to choose among several perfectly nourishing items on a restaurant menu, except where matters of expense or diet might be involved. But anything, even apparently trivial or routine, may become a matter of spiritual importance under certain circumstances. Everything which has a bearing on a person's effectiveness as a witness, down to the details of his clothing and personal habits, *may* become subject to decision in the light of God's leading.

Everything is theoretically possible with God, according to the apologists for the view we are considering, but in order to achieve his purpose he has to grant men freedom either to cooperate or to refuse to cooperate with him. A divine victory based on necessity would not satisfy him. But a divine victory secured by the persuasion of free spirits who voluntarily choose fellowship rather than rebellion and antagonism is a spiritually satisfying victory. God could have created and maintained a universe in which everything happened according to his *fiat*. However, he chose to create and maintain a system in which there is a gradation of processes, at one end of the scale automatic, at the other end of the scale autonomous. This inevitably means that, if responsible beings deliberately choose to do wrong, God suffers the *divine counterpart* of disappointment and suffering. When, in the fulfillment of his plan for the salvation of man, he sent his Son into the world, he doomed himself to *something like* emotional agony on an infinite scale. But since he may be thought of, as Thomas Aquinas suggested, as having *conpassio* for the world, but not as experiencing *passio,* religiously it is right to conceive of God as solicitous and loving, as disappointed with us when we fail him, as glad when we trust and obey him, always recognizing that our earthbound spirits cannot compass or fathom the Eternal Spirit.

If God knows what is happening everywhere, if he knows of someone whom we could help who is not immediately present with us, and if he can communicate with us because we are made in his spiritual "image," there is no incongruity in the idea that we can receive guidance from him about another person at a distance. Frank Buchman himself claims to have been "guided" to get off a train and return to his point of departure to help someone in a hotel-room near the station, and to find a desperate man about to commit suicide, a tragedy he was able to prevent. He has been "led" to leave a meeting at a camp and go to a certain cabin, there to find one of the delegates suffering from acute appendicitis. He has been "guided" to go out on a street in Hartford, there to meet face to face a man whom he had helped the day before, and who had been intensely desirous of seeing him again. This sort of thing takes place with most of those who live their lives on the basis of a constant seeking for divine direction.

God is thought of as dictating significant words, phrases, sometimes whole sentences, to those who observe a "quiet time" of uninterrupted "listening" in the early morning. These divine messages can be written down in a book and used for guidance during the day. I do not mean that the morning is the only time when this can happen, but that the quiet and freshness of that time of day, when one turns his mind to God and waits expectantly for help, seems to be peculiarly productive. Sometimes the phrases or names which come into the mind do not mean anything to the recipient at first; but they serve to alert him as to what to recognize as significant later on.

An example of this was given to me in private conversation: the word "Albany" flashed into a man's mind as he was observing his early "quiet time." The luminosity of this thought convinced him that the Lord was preparing his mind to be ready to respond to something or someone associated with Albany. Shortly afterwards, a yacht pulled into the harbor of the town in which he was vacationing. He happened to be on the dock when the wife of the owner asked him if he could tell her how she could get her husband to a drug store. In offering the service of his automobile, a natural point of contact was established. The couple were from *Albany.* The husband was suffering from alcoholism. The wife told the man who had had the flash of inspiration about "Albany" that their doctor at home had urged them to get into touch with the group of which he was a member. The result was a facing up to the issues of life, a renunciation of drink on the part of the husband, and a surrender of both man and wife to God's will in Christ.

Guidance is thought to be given about what to believe. The truth of Christianity is dependent on revelation. The

Spirit of God tells those who read the Bible with an open mind and a receptive heart that what they are reading is the true Word. Religious belief cannot be thought of as something that is arrived at by induction at the end of a long process of reasoning. Belief in the Christian God is a revelation by the Holy Spirit to those who are in the proper frame of mind. Therefore, when Arnold Bennett, as one writer in a series on religion, stated: "I do not believe, and never have at any time believed, in the divinity of Christ, the Virgin birth, . . . heaven, hell, the immortality of the soul, the divine inspiration of the Bible"—and thereby drew down upon his head a veritable avalanche of ecclesiastical criticism—an Oxford group member said that to attack him was wrong because he was honest, and obviously expressing his true opinion; and that one could not expect anything else from a man who had not been "born again." Under guidance, a surrendered soul would receive confirmation of the truths of revealed religion.

Guidance is also, of course, the supreme source of illumination on moral matters. Humanly thought-out morality is apt to be purely prudential. "Guided" morality is on an entirely different basis. Certain definite norms or principles were revealed in the life and teaching of Jesus. His requirements have been often summed up, in the evangelical tradition, as absolute honesty, absolute purity, absolute unselfishness, absolute love. But the Christian life cannot be based on a mere logical application of these principles, as if they represented a new legalism which covers all the variety of necessary moral choices. The active Spirit of God is their interpreter to the mind of the believer. Historical revelation is the guarantee that ethical guidance shall not be subject to the vagaries of purely personal taste. The freely given guidance of God, which comes at a time of genuine and willing receptivity, can be distinguished from mere whim by checking it against basic Christian principles. If it satisfies these conditions, it may be acted upon safely as divine.

Another way to check it is against the guidance of other surrendered people. On the whole, the leading given to one consecrated person is very much like that vouchsafed to another. On certain minor matters, like smoking or moderate drinking, there is apt to be a difference in guidance for different individuals; but most of those who base their lives consciously on the view of God's direction which we are considering have given up tobacco and alcohol completely. All are led to a strict, orthodox, Christian standard of sexual morality. If one is dubious about a course of action, the injunction is, in the words of the old hymn, "Take it to the Lord in prayer." The conviction is that one should be able to take God into every nook and cranny of his life without a twinge of conscience; and if one's thoughts, words, or acts in any way make one feel uncomfortable when God is recognized as present, this is evidence of sin and compromise. The clear conscience on ordinary moral matters is a testimony to the guided life. No humble Christian can claim to maintain a clear conscience constantly, for we are all sinners; but the sensitive response to God's direction is the best possible way to achieve as much clarity as can humanly be realized. We are always "compromising" with absolute standards, but the believer in divine guidance feels that if an action is actually the best that could possibly be done in a given situation, the Lord can tell the surrendered person about it, and if it is performed, it is not a "compromise."

The sex problem can be directed by God in all its details. Continence before marriage and fidelity afterwards is considered the only regime which fits in with the divine plan. One cannot take God into a situation where there is the slightest hint of un-Christian sexual indulgence. A man cannot be guided to engage in physical familiarities with a woman whom he does not intend to marry; nor can a guided woman allow intimacies of any sort with a man to whom she is not engaged. God may suggest the person one should marry, or confirm the suggestion submitted to him in "quiet time." A truly Christian engagement is a "guided" engagement. Marriage is a relationship not between two but among three; God should be considered the indispensable third party in any true wedlock. If one's married partner becomes incapable of sex expression, the supernaturally directed answer to the problem would be that the other sublimate his desires rather than have recourse to divorce or extra-marital satisfaction. A guided sex-life would never be a repressed one. God can take care of repression by the redirection of energy. Nor should there be anything joyless in all this; sex is a heaven-sent capacity to love and to procreate, and can be enjoyed as the expression of a spiritual relationship between two married people.

God provides for the physical wants of true believers. He uses guidance to stir the minds of those with money to give to those who do not have it. Many people who give full-time to evangelistic work live "on faith" and God never fails them, for other surrendered people with jobs or incomes share generously what they possess. All property belongs to God, who has lent a share of it to each of us as a steward. If we are in touch with him, and are willing to be guided in how we use our resources, he will tell us the best use to make of them. He will guide us as to how much to spend on ourselves, how much to save, how much to give to charity.

Sometimes, of course, people have told about their experiences in this realm in terms which cause the raised eyebrow and the skeptical smile from the unsympathetic. An advertising man once told of how he was guided to give to his business partner a check for an estimated discrepancy in an expense account which he had turned in before his conversion. "Then," he writes, "as miracles began to happen, God guided me to the discovery of a check I had folded up, put away and forgotten—made out to me for the exact amount he had guided me to give to my partner." [1] "The most remarkable result" of his God-guided life was, he says, that although his attempt to apply the standard of absolute honesty to the advertising business had reduced his financial rewards, "all anxiety and fear have flown out the window never to return." God told him during his "quiet time" one morning to "make no plans for the evening but to be on hand and ready to seize the opportunity that *would* arise." And the opportunity came, evidently in the form of some advertising business.[2] God also guided him to invest his money in an enterprise which turned out to be lucrative, and left him freer than ever to engage in various "phases of creative spiritual activity."

Naturally, this whole business can be the occasion for vagaries that seem superstitious and childish. When once the business is started of swapping experiences of guidance in a group meeting, a number of rather dubious examples are likely to be cited. The same thing happens with after-dinner stories of weird encounters with the supernatural. Someone always knows of someone else who has had inexplicable messages from the beyond, or who has *seen* a person who later on turns out to have been dead at the time. Marvellous stories of being led out of situations of physical danger are apt to be told in guidance-sharing sessions; lost articles have been found through God's direction; the true likeness of Christ has been revealed to a painter by the Holy Spirit; movers have been secured in October in a city where ordinarily one has to sign them up months in advance because God wished a family to take advantage of a fortunate opportunity to rent a new apartment. But it is not fair to cite the weird and peripheral in any movement as an example of what it leads to, especially when aberrations are frowned upon by the more sober members.

All this has been part of the evangelical Protestant tradition, in its more "enthusiastic" and mystical forms, for a long, long time. I remember as a boy in Toronto hearing my mother tell of a man who rang our doorbell and said, "The Lord sent me to you. I need money desperately." Mother replied that she was terribly sorry to have to turn him down, but that the Lord always warned her in advance of an approaching "touch." Something in the man's bearing apparently suggested to my mother that he was using pious language to disarm the suspicion that he was a plain panhandler.

The contemporary believers in divine guidance are sometimes Fundamentalist, but very often "liberal" to the extent that they accept the scientific criticism of the Bible. They believe that, humanly speaking, we are animals with an evolutionary history. Henry Drummond of Scotland, a believer in guidance and one of the most effective evangelists of his day—he died in 1897—was a scientist and an evolutionist. But he believed that the moment mankind was endowed with self-awareness, and the ability to stand off and look at itself, moral responsibility became real. Many modern Protestants agree with him that a soul has the capacity to transcend the purely physiological aspects of the evolutionary process and respond to ideals, to other souls, and to God. It is admitted that there are certain "natural" tendencies, which have stood the species in good stead during its early struggle for existence but which the soul must now suppress or sublimate. In some cases this cannot be done unless the personality is strengthened by an influx of divine power, one might almost say "from without," except that such an expression makes use of a spatial category which is inapplicable to the spiritual world. So, for good and sufficient reasons from God's point of view, man is doomed to a struggle between his selfish, animal nature and his God-given, spiritual nature. His ordinary nature derives from a physiological evolutionary process and is continually offering him suggestions as to how to satisfy the normal cravings of the "natural" man. And some of these are permissible, as they drive in the direction of self-preservation and self-propagation. But there is much in human nature that has to be transcended; and most contemporary theologians affirm it is *not only* our evolutionary inheritance that causes sin. However we came by it, there is in man a desire to be completely his own master, to set himself up as God, to affirm his life over against other life, a tendency so deeply rooted as to have suggested to many thinkers that he shares in "original sin." This is not merely the propensity to commit "sins," of the flesh or even of the spirit, but the dreadful inclination to rebel against what God would do to help him and save him. Men need to be *reborn,* not *reformed.* Re-birth can only follow surrender to God in Christ. Upon surrender, the soul can become the recipient of supernatural illumination (as to what is right) and supernatural power (to do what is right). The victory over sin is never complete in this life. The guided life is hard, not easy. But, if guidance is conscientiously followed, in spite of unpopularity, misunderstanding, privation and discouragement, the peace and joy which pass all understanding will be given freely by God. The Cross then becomes a symbol not only of the struggle against the powers of darkness, but also of the victory over them.

We have seen that all Christians who believe that God somehow guides us, whether through communion or in more specific ways through communication, believe that prayer, as an opening-up of the heart and mind to the influence of the Divine, is the key to the religious life. Prayer involves not only praise and petition, confession and repentance, but also meditation and sincere "listening" for what God has to say, however this is thought of as taking place. The more recent apologists for divine guidance conceive that it is "not God's way to drop ideas into our mind as one drops pebbles into a pond." Dr. L. D. Weatherhead, for example, says we ought to check the tendency to think of the uncanny as the Divine, or to feel that detailed guidance comes by some weird clairvoyant process unrelated to the ordinary workings of the mind. All normal processes can be used by God to transmit his messages to us, and there is no reason for believing that there is a sharp distinction between what "comes" to us by one method or another. The main thing is that God should be loved and served and obeyed all the days of our lives, and that the activity of our own minds, in our busy-ness and preoccupation, should never be so hectic and constant as to leave no room for him to make his will known to us, and to allow no unhurried opportunity for communion with him, and communication from him. With these sentiments all evangelical Christians should agree.

CHAPTER 7

The God of Cults and Sects

THE newspapers now urge us all to worship on Sunday at a church of our choice. If one looks at a New York newspaper on a Saturday morning, one is bound to be impressed by the wideness of that choice. In addition to the usual evangelical Protestant services (Baptist, Congregational, Disciples, Lutheran, Dutch Reformed, Methodist, Presbyterian, Protestant Episcopal), one finds non-denominational churches, a "Liberal Catholic" service, a Glad Tidings Tabernacle, many Christian Science gatherings, together with announcements of Baha'i, Church of Divine Unity, Church of the Healing Christ, The Science of Religion, Ethical Culture, Spiritualist Science, Spiritualist, Swedenborgian, Theosophist, Unity, Greater Truth Society, Hinduism, Vedanta, and Yoga. One expects to see the hours of Roman Catholic masses at the Cathedral listed, as well as the services at Temple Emmanu-el and the Unitarian and Universalist Churches, but then he finds a Jewish Science group to match the Christian Science fellowship. We rightly glory in our heritage of freedom of worship, but a visitor from another planet might wonder if that freedom is not being somewhat overdone! It *is* encouraging to know that the movement for church unity is making definite if slow progress and that new sects are not proliferating as they did in the past. But one cannot help wondering what God thinks of it all; for in all these sanctuaries the Deity is worshipped, each congregation feeling that its approach is the one which does the greatest justice to the mystery of the Divine. The conception of God officially held by a group may have *something* in common with that held by several others, but it is difficult to see where there would be any common denominator at all under many of them.

I have had some personal acquaintance with the adherents of most sects. I have even attended meetings of some groups no longer listed in the papers, like the League for the Larger Life (which has apparently disbanded). I have known Mormons, Seventh-Day Adventists, and Jehovah's Witnesses. To me the contrasting theologies of these sects are fascinating. Since we have already examined the beliefs of many groups in the main stream of our tradition, we shall now glance at the Church of Jesus Christ of the Latter-day Saints, the Seventh-Day Adventists, the Spiritualists (or Spiritists, as the unsympathetic prefer to call them), the group popularly known as Jehovah's Witnesses, the Theosophical Movement, and Christian Science. I apologize to the representatives of these fellowships for seeming to classify them together. I do not mean to do so. I am only looking at them one after the other, in one chapter, without implying that they have anything in common, either by way of tradition or significance, except their deviation from the ordinarily accepted tenets of evangelical Christianity. Specifically, I am concerned with their views of God, and I shall try to restrict my presentation of their history and characteristics to those features which help to make their theology clear.

The Latter-day Saints believe that the Christian Gospel existed before creation, that it was revealed to the very first human beings, that mankind was guilty of apostasy from it (God's answer to this unfaithfulness was the Flood), and that it has had to be proclaimed to the world again in various dispensations (through Abraham, Moses and others). The final "restoration" of the truth occurred early in the last century, through Joseph Smith's discovery of the Book of Mormon, a translation of which he spent two years dictating to scribes who sat on the other side of a screen. Among other things, these sacred writings sanctioned plural marriage, which was soon practiced by many of Smith's followers, and which aroused such antagonism among the God-fearing Protestants of New York, Ohio, and, later, Illinois that, after Smith and his brother were killed by a mob, Brigham Young was forced to lead the group farther and farther West, until they reached the Great Salt Lake, and settled down. In 1890 they officially gave up polygamy, and Utah was admitted to the Union five years later.

Mormons accept Joseph Smith as a prophet of God, as well as his successors from Brigham Young to the present president of the Church, although there are a few splinter-groups, each claiming to be Smith's true spiritual descendents.

The Latter-day Saints have an almost tritheistic conception of the Trinity, accepting the Godhead as three literal, distinct personalities: God the Father; Jesus Christ the Son (one with the Father in purpose and thought, separate in "physical fact"); [1] and the Holy Ghost, a spiritual Personage. They place great stress on a God who made his children "in his own image"; Jesus is "the express image of his person" (Hebrews 1:3). They believe in the atoning sacrifice of Christ and his literal resurrection from the dead; he is the Savior of mankind, who is coming back again to rule the earth. The Book of Mormon is *not* the "Bible" of the Latter-day Saints, but only a supplement to the Christian Bible; the King James version is preferred and is accepted as the Word of God "as far as it can be translated correctly."

Energy, matter and mind are all thought of as having existed from eternity, and as being indestructible. Man himself pre-existed, and will live forever. There will be a resurrection of all from the dead on the appointed day. Everyone will eventually be "saved," although there will be "degrees of glory" in the after-life; and "heaven" is considered to be a place where families will be reunited, and progress can be made. The Mormons baptize by immersion, celebrate the Lord's Supper by means of bread and water (not wine), and confirm those wishing to join the church by a simple "laying on of hands." Baptism is "vicariously" undertaken by the living for those who have died without the proper opportunity to hear and accept the word. The Latter-day Saints are enthusiastic missionaries, whose labors have been instrumental in establishing well over three thousand congregations throughout the world. They are thrifty people, who devote at least one-tenth of their income to the work of their Church. Their code of health and conduct, promulgated in 1833, requires abstinence from all "injurious substances," including tobacco, liquor, and *hot* coffee and tea, but approves the enjoyment of wholesome food and beverages in a spirit of temperance and gratitude. They believe in the cardinal virtues of honor, truthfulness, chastity, and benevolence, and feel that the best way to show their devotion to a Just and Loving God is by serving their fellow men.

Those unsympathetic with Mormonism call attention to practices which present-day believers tend to soft-pedal or omit entirely, such as the "celestial marriage," supposed to be binding throughout the after-life.[2] They also emphasize such weird beliefs, found in the official literature, as the one that Jesus married Martha and two Marys, thus providing a New Testament sanction for polygamy, and that Jesus' Davidic descent comes through Bathsheba, illustrating the notion that if David had not been a polygamist, there would have been no Messiah. Furthermore, there is some evidence that Mormons have believed that they alone will inherit eternal life, although it is only fair to point out that the adherents of most sects have at times been guilty of what we might call such eschatological exclusiveness.

In any case, we must admit that this is a strange religion to anyone steeped in traditional evangelical Christianity. The Book of Mormon itself seems like an incredible pastiche of quotations from sources much later than its supposed date of composition. The somewhat tritheistic godhead vouchsafes "revelations" which modify or supersede the traditional scriptures, and uses men of great force but dubious character for the transmission of the message. If the present attitude of many Mormon leaders reflects a modification of certain tenets of the faith, then God is not one who will condemn anyone to everlasting punishment, but here again the evidence is inconclusive. Mormons claim to be "Christians" but not "Protestants." They claim that Joseph Smith, a member of no church, received a direct revelation from the Father of Our Lord Jesus Christ to "restore" the true faith among men. God today, therefore, is far more interested in the million and a half Latter-day Saints than in all the rest of humanity, and looks upon this contemporary Restoration as akin in importance to the dispensations begun with Abraham and Moses and the earthly Jesus. Their view of the Deity effectively precludes any intimate theological rapport with those in the ordinary Protestant tradition. What the Roman Church thinks of the Mormons does not need to be made explicit!

The Seventh-day Adventists claim to be the only Christian group which has remained completely faithful to the Bible in observing the Sabbath on the seventh rather than the first day of the week. They expect the return of Christ to earth soon, and they believe it is their duty to warn the world of this expectation. They apparently feel that only 144,000 elect will inherit eternal life, but they are quite sure of their own place among this number.[3] They classify themselves as Protestants, as having direct access to God without any intermediaries, and as the rediscoverers of ancient truths long obscured by the importation of pagan notions into the teaching of the more conventional denominations. They claim never to have found any New Testament authority for changing the weekly day of rest to Sunday, and they take the Bible literally at all points, including the belief that God created the world in six days of twenty-four hours each.

William Miller was the founder of the Adventists. In 1831, he predicted that, on the basis of his study of Daniel and Revelation, the Second Coming of Christ would take place before 1843 was out. When this did not happen, he revised his estimate and foretold that it would in 1844; when this hope also was disappointed, he gave up, and Ellen Harmon White took over, establishing the movement under its present name and with its present emphasis. She and her followers held the view that "the Lord did really come in 1844, not to the earth, but to cleanse the sanctuary in Heaven. . . . The Lord passed into the sanctuary in 1844" (apparently he had only been in the outer court since the resurrection). She claimed to have been "taken up into Heaven and shown" this amazing sight. Immediately after this, the Lord was believed to have closed the "door of mercy to sinners," initiating the Final Judgment. Only those who knew about this could benefit by Christ's mediation. That other Christians worship on Sunday is called "The Mark of the Beast"; only those who observe the true Biblical custom of the sabbath, and who *also* accept Christ as their personal Savior will share, as the elect, in the future glory of God. Mrs. White had a heavenly vision corroborating this insistence on the seventh day as holy. She was transported spiritually to the realms above and, as she watched, Jesus raised the cover of the ark, and she beheld the tables of stone on which the Ten Commandments were written. She was amazed as she saw the Fourth Commandment in the very center of the ten precepts, with a soft halo of light encircling it.

The Adventists affirm that the Second Coming will be the climax of a series of tremendous, earth-shaking events. The followers of Christ who have already died and who sleep in silence, as the dead were thought to rest in Sheol in Old Testament times, will be resurrected, and along with the faithful among the living will reign with him for a thousand years (Revelation 20:4). This millennium will be in *heaven* rather than on earth; during this period the earth will be a "desolate, depopulated wilderness." However, after this is over, the wicked who have been asleep during this time will be raised, the righteous will return from heaven, and the New Jerusalem will be set up on our planet for the faithful, with final judgment pronounced upon the unfaithful and wicked.

The conception of God in Seventh-day Adventism is of a Triune Power who is both Judge of the nations and Savior of his elect. He insists upon strict and puritanical standards of conduct. He commissions many to act as missionaries to bring the saving knowledge to others. Christ is thought of as having been kept on the threshold of the sanctuary in heaven until 1844 and then as having gone in to cleanse it, and to prepare it for the millennium. God is conceived as reserving places in heaven and, later, in the heaven on earth, for a relatively small number of the human race. There is nothing much in this type of belief to attract the average Protestant.

The Spiritualists hold services every Sunday in New York and many other parts of the country and the world, as well as midweek meetings and special séances. They believe firmly that the spirits of the departed can communicate with the living through mediums, people specially gifted with a certain kind of receptivity, and sensitive to messages from the other world. The movement received a baptism of respectability in England when Sir Oliver Lodge, the great physicist, and Sir Arthur Conan Doyle, the creator of Sherlock Holmes, became interested in it and were convinced of the possibility of spiritistic communion with the dead. Lord Dowding, former chief of the Royal Air Force, is a present-day believer. The British Society for Psychical Research has published an impressive series of volumes of "proceedings," describing all sorts of experiences in the field, some of them extraordinarily difficult to explain on any other basis than the one the Spiritualists accept. The central tenet of their creed is naturally of intense interest to many people; almost everyone knows of those who have had startling encounters with the occult; and during the twentieth century, marked as it has been by the most devastating wars of all time and a threat of the destruction of our civilization as we know it, it is not at all surprising that the movement should continue to thrive, even on a somewhat modest scale numerically. With human life occupying such a precarious position on a minor planet in the midst of awesome star-studded space, many are anxious to know something about the continued existence of the soul after death, and know it more definitely than is possible for those who merely profess faith in it without any detailed proof.

Although there has been an interest in communication with the dead since time immemorial, the modern movement began in Hydeville, New York, in 1847, with the circulation of stories about the mysterious experiences of two young girls, the Fox sisters, who believed that the souls of the departed answered their questions by means of rappings, three raps being interpreted as "yes," one rap as "no," two raps as "doubtful." The neighborhood was fascinated by what the children were doing, and many became convinced that the responses received represented the activity of disembodied spirits in the after-life seeking to break through into this. Margaret and Kate Fox were pronounced to be "mediums." Others held séances and sittings; soon the movement was well under way. In 1882, a group of scientifically minded people, skeptical but not unreceptive, formed the Society for Psychical Research, whose American proceedings parallel in interest if not in prestige the later investigations of the British branch. From the very beginning the Society abroad attracted more distinguished men of science and letters than here; and in America the appearance of mediums who made a good deal of money from the conduct of séances brought the subject into general disrepute. But Spiritualism (or Spiritism, as the critics prefer to call it) still is a force to be reckoned with and represents a steady challenge to the disbelief in immortality characteristic of the mind-set of many scientists and members of the intelligentsia.

It is not a "Christian" movement, and it does not seem to yield any important insights on theological or religious matters. Communion with those who have passed on—yes; communion with God—no! By implication God does not seem to be particularly interested in man, and man's interest in God is conceived as chiefly speculative. For the Christian, God represents the chief ground for his hope of life beyond the grave; for the Spiritualist (if we are to take the communications received from the dead as any indication) God is something of an afterthought; there have even been British philosophers who believed in immortality while disbelieving in God. In Christian theology, it is faith in the nature and character of God which sustains the belief in life eternal. It has been said that Spiritualism was born not so much out of trust in God as of distrust in him. The faithful follower of Jesus seems not at all interested in spending time and energy and money and concern on proving that there is some sort of survival of bodily death. He is perfectly willing to let the nature of the future life dawn upon him when the time comes; "one world at a time" is his motto. But he is a believer as truly as the Spiritualist.

The dead are thought of as communicating with the living not directly but generally through a "control," an experienced spirit in the world beyond, who transmits their messages through a medium in a trance during a séance in a darkened room. Normally, therefore, my dead father would not find it possible to speak to me directly. He, in the after-life, would have to find a "control." I, in this life, would seek out a medium. But the medium cannot just "listen," as an Oxford grouper would listen for a message from God. The medium must go into a trance. Then the "control," having received my father's message to me must use the now unconscious medium, especially the medium's vocal equipment, to transmit it. Practically, there are many difficulties. My father may not have given the message with complete accuracy, or the "control" may have misunderstood my father, or may prefer to phrase the message in his own way. The medium may have an off-day. Or there may be some interference with communication and reception. And I may misunderstand the message. It is all rather strange and difficult. Every now and then, however, messages will come through with remarkable clarity, and will carry conviction. For instance, the whereabouts of an important document, apparently known to no one living but known to one recently deceased, will be conveyed through a medium in a séance, and the truth of the message will be confirmed by the discovery. This sort of thing has happened scores of times. Into the intricacies of these matters it is not my intention to go, nor into the elaborate ways in which the skeptics explain them without reference to the action of departed spirits. But the bulk of what comes through from the other world seems, when one studies it, to be vague, imprecise and not terribly important. Furthermore, as has been remarked more than once, messages purporting to come from someone who was very intelligent during his earthly life more often than not betray a sad deterioration in mentality. A formerly bright person communicates something dull; a perspicacious individual transmits a cliché. This is very discouraging.

I should not be writing about the Spiritualists at all because I am somewhat prejudiced against what they believe. I once took part, under the direction of Houdini, in a public exposé of some of the methods used in séances. But I am concerned with the implied theology of the movement. The picture one gets, by putting the pieces of the spirit-messages together, is that we are born into this world, we live, we pass into the next, and we are guaranteed a place in the future kingdom simply because of our indestructible humanity. Nothing is made of a God who judges; nothing is heard of a Savior who saves. A person who has left a trail of broken lives in his wake on earth conceivably would suffer from the realization, either sudden or gradual, of the harm for which he has been responsible. This would be "hell" for an individual with any conscience at all. Contrariwise, a person who "went about doing good" on earth might experience a feeling of satisfaction in the next, if more information than he had on earth about the beneficial results of his charity were vouchsafed to him. But this is all problematical, even in Spiritualistic terms, and is certainly very different from the Christian concept of eternal life with God, who is both Judge and Father. The Spiritualist picture of life beyond the grave may seem to some more definite than that of those who merely believe in immortality, leaving aside others who have been taught what to think about heaven and hell and any intermediate state there may be. But the picture still leaves many questions unanswered.

Lady Conan Doyle once received a message from a control in the spirit world named Pheneas. The message read: "Your home in the other world is ready for you. There is a small round building in the grounds which is filled with exquisite colored vibrations into which you go when you want your soul's rejuvenation. . . . There is an oblong pond round which colored birds come to drink."[4] One wishes to know many things: *where* is this? What kind of astral bodies will we have with eyes to enjoy the colors? Why will our souls need rejuvenation? What about the birds? Is this all in a non-spatial realm of some sort? What about time? Do we know more about God there than we do here? If the life beyond is to be nothing more than a garden-suburb of much the same kind that we see in Westchester or Connecticut, it is not very much like that the saints have hoped for.

It may be that this is what we are in for. It may be that our desperate search for a satisfying concept of God will *not* be rewarded in the hereafter. It may be, as Spiritualist revelations imply, that we will know no more of the Divine in the next life than we do in this. But if, after devoting years to the study of the *Proceedings,* and hours upon hours to sittings and mediums, we receive no more satisfying answers than the devotees of this movement now have, we may well feel that we have been cheated. The ordinary evangelical Christian believes that if we have genuine faith in God as he reveals himself in Christ, we can safely leave the *details* of the future in his hands, confident that, in his concern for what is truly best for us, he will show that concern in some form of life everlasting.

From time to time, a pair of earnest, attractive people, a man and a woman, but not married, ring our doorbell and sell us copies of *The Watchtower* (*Announcing Jehovah's Kingdom*) and *Awake,* issued by the *Watch Tower Bible and Tract Society of Pennsylvania,* whose headquarters are in Brooklyn. We find these magazines very interesting indeed. They are the official publications of the group known as Jehovah's Witnesses, who take their name from the verse in Isaiah 43:12: "Ye are my witnesses, saith Jehovah, that I am God." They are not a denomination, or an incorporated body. Members are simply associated with the publication society, which determines the strategy and emphasis of the movement. It has become widely known through its tract-sellers, its spectacular public gatherings (the members regularly fill the Yankee Stadium for their yearly convocation), its opposition to conscription and war, and its refusal to sanction blood-transfusions.

The idea behind it originated in the mind of Charles Taze Russell of Pittsburgh in 1872, who was stimulated at the age of twenty by reading the writings of a group of Second Adventists. Russell inherited five haberdashery stores from his father, but he sold these in order to devote all his time to the spread of his religious ideas. His literary output was tremendous. In addition to a magazine which he edited and largely wrote himself, and the preparation of scores of tracts, he produced a seven-volume *Studies in the Scriptures,* which sets forth the views of the *Witnesses* and is considered normative as an interpretation of the Bible. However, it is a literal belief in the Old and New Testaments which determines the character of their religious life. When Russell died in 1916, Judge Rutherford succeeded him as the head of the movement, and remained president of the Watch Tower Society until his death in 1942. The movement has spread all over the world. It was even banned as subversive by the governments of New Zealand and Australia during World War II. It is run by a central Board of Directors, which keeps strict control of the elaborate organization of magazine vendors, who distribute the tracts, and record-salesmen, who distribute the recordings of Judge Rutherford's sermons. The representatives I have met have always impressed me with their sincerity, enthusiasm and devotion, even though I find it impossible to agree with their theology, sociology or politics.

Though the Witnesses subscribe to none of the classical creeds of Christendom, they believe in Jehovah as the only true God. It was Satan who challenged the Deity's supremacy, who caused the defection of Adam and Eve in Eden, and who continues to conduct an active campaign of opposition to the Most High. In the course of time, God found it necessary to send his Son into the world to be a sacrifice for the sins of men, and to break the power of Satan.

The beginning of the end for the Devil came, according to the Witnesses, in 1914, when Christ assumed his Kingly power in heaven. His first act was to throw Satan out of paradise. Satan then began his systematic disruption of all the settled moralities of civilized men, resulting in wars, revolutions, the increase of disbelief and libertinism, and the degradation of arts and manners. This period in which we are now living will be climaxed by the war of Armageddon, in which the Devil and all his henchmen will be defeated, and Christ's Millennium will be established.

The Godhead is not conceived as a Trinity; there is no need in their theology for a Holy Spirit; there is simply Jehovah and Christ, who are two distinct persons. Jehovah created Christ before anything else, and then, in turn, in Jehovah's name, Christ created the world. There seem to be some curious subsidiary doctrines which Russell set forth, but which do not appear in the Witnesses' contemporary publications, such as that, before his incarnation Jesus was, for a time, the Archangel Michael, and that during his earthly sojourn he gave up his angelic nature and became a fallible mortal. Nevertheless, his sacrifice was sufficient to win for man a chance of glory and immortality, and the opportunity to work out his own salvation. Jesus, at his death, received a new spiritual body in which he rose (his earthly body having been removed supernaturally from the tomb). The function of the Risen Christ is as the Executive Officer of Jehovah. All human beings cease to live conscious lives at death, but at the Second Advent of Christ, when he ushers in the Millennium, all the dead will be revived, raised, and given another chance. Rutherford taught that "Eternal torture is void of the principle of love. God is Love. A Creator that would torture his creatures eternally would be a fiend, and not a God of love." [5] The nature of life in the Millennium has been pictured in some detail in the literature of the Witnesses, but their current preaching seems to stress chiefly the simple message of hope for the human race. Death and hell (which is a place of unconsciousness, something like the Old Testament Sheol) will both be destroyed at the end of the Millennium. Only 144,000 (see Revelation 7:4) will inherit the Kingdom of God *in heaven*. The rest of humanity will live *forever on earth*.

The Witnesses practice baptism by immersion for entrance into full-fledged membership. All members are commissioned to preach and proclaim; the "priesthood of all believers" is affirmed, and clerical garb is never used. Youths are invited to preach, following the Biblical examples of Samuel, Jeremiah, and Timothy, as well as that of the twelve-year-old Jesus, who discussed the Scriptures with the pundits of his day.

Members of the movement quote Leviticus 17:10 and Acts 15:20 in substantiation of their refusal to receive blood transfusions. Leviticus warns against eating "any manner of blood"; James in the Acts orders all followers of Jesus to "abstain from blood." The Witnesses see no difference between allowing an injection of blood and consuming blood by mouth.

They will not salute the flag, as this seems to them like worshipping a non-religious symbol. Although they believe that the wars of the Israelites in Bible times were God's wars and therefore permissible, nowadays no nation is truly a theocratic state and therefore its secular international conflicts are not holy. There should be no call for a Witness to put allegiance to his government ahead of allegiance to God by fighting in modern wars. Furthermore, since ministers of religion in most civilized countries are excused from active military service, the Witnesses, all of whom claim to be ministers, feel that they should be also.

Thus we have another group who are, in a sense, "in" the world but not "of" it. They believe that Jehovah revealed himself in a Bible which should be literally interpreted, and whose prophecies should be taken seriously as applying to the twentieth century. Although some of their leader's remarks about God seem somewhat *bi*nitarian (Jehovah and Christ being considered completely distinct personalities, each with his own self-conscious ego), it probably would be fairer to classify them as strong and convinced monotheists, with Jesus being considered an agent of God, superior to man, but not "substantially" divine. The Witnesses surely know their Bibles. From the standpoint of modern Biblical criticism, they seem to misinterpret or take at its face value much that should be understood historically or symbolically. But no one can deny that the movement consists in the main of sober, faithful, God-fearing adherents, obedient to what they believe are the commandments of a stern yet loving Deity.

When we come to consider Theosophy, we move into an entirely different realm. Here we find the western form of an Eastern view of life, acknowledging its spiritual indebtedness not to the Bible, but to the Hindu Upanishads and the Buddhist writings. Some of the most interesting people I have ever known are Theosophists, extraordinarily creative in the realm of the arts, and devoted to the pursuit of truth, goodness and beauty. The movement has roots which run way back to the beginnings of the Christian era and beyond, but the modern version of it began with the formation of the Theosophical Society in New York, in 1875, by Madame H. P. Blavatsky and Colonel H. S. Olcott. The cultural climate of America did not seem congenial to Madame Blavatsky, so she went to India, studied the writings of many Eastern mystics, and finally produced the book, *Secret Doctrine,* which is the "catechism of modern Theosophy."[6] It was Mrs. Annie Besant's systematization of the teaching of this volume that commended it to the kind of cultured and creative people who now are numbered among its adherents.

I remember once visiting an American men's college and attending a very popular class on "The Eastern View of Life," taught by a professor from India. I could not help being amused at the sight of those undergraduates, many of them in heavy sweaters decorated with varsity letters, solemnly taking notes on the transmigration of souls and ontological mysticism. How could they ever enter sympathetically into the world-view they were studying? Could they get even a glimpse of its inner meaning let alone an understanding of its hold on millions of people in the East? For the basic value-judgment of classical Hinduism is that being a self-conscious individual is in itself undesirable, and that the *summum bonum* of life would be to lose one's sense of selfhood. The endless cycle of incarnation and reincarnation as distinct centers of self-awareness appears evil; the goal would be to break the cycle and to be poured back into the great undifferentiated pool of Being. Oriental mysticism means the losing of the self in God; occidental communion means the intensification of genuine selfhood by being used by God for the carrying out of his purposes. At this point the chasm between East and West seems very great indeed.

Contemporary Theosophists belong to the Orient rather than the Occident in their basic evaluation of individualism, although they do not express their desire to be rid of the self in such extreme terms as do many Eastern thinkers. Actually, the ones I have known are inventive, creative and extraordinarily singular. Each one stands out as an individual on this planet, and takes an active part in the cultural life of our day. But their basic assumptions about the meaning of life and especially the ultimate destiny of the race are Eastern rather than Western.

For instance, they use language which smacks strongly of pantheism: "All that is is God, and God is all that is." And yet they also say that God "created" everything we see, and "wills" its continued existence: statements which sound suspiciously like personalistic theism.[7] They try to reconcile this apparent conflict by affirming that God is *supra-personal,* not just personal. They look upon personality as a limitation unworthy of the divine; this is, of course, in line with the oriental yearning to transcend self-awareness, which God supremely does. God is really impersonal Justice, even though he is spoken of at times as "loving" and "truthful." But to employ such terms is to be poetical rather than metaphysical; these expressions belong to the life of devotion rather than of philosophical speculation.

Mrs. Besant reverenced Jesus as one of the Masters of the spiritual life, although she seems to have invented a biography for him which departs completely from the Gospel account. According to her, Christ was born about one hundred years before the date we have settled on as the beginning of the Christian era. He got his training among the Essenes, and imbibed the secret wisdom of India and Egypt from visiting teachers. After his death, he returned for a period of fifty years to instruct his intimate followers. He was the divine Christ only from the baptism to the crucifixion; so an historically rooted Christology receives no help from this theosophical interpretation.

Of course, the feature of Theosophy which has always excited the most interest and caused the most controversy is the belief in the transmigration of souls. If a person lives for the things of the spirit in any incarnation, his soul, at his death, will be transplanted into the body of someone newly born who will enjoy a higher spiritual status than the one enjoyed in the previous incarnation. If, on the other hand, anyone abuses his opportunities, commits a crime, lives chiefly for the flesh, his soul at death will be *demoted,* as it were, in the scale of being, so that he will be forced to exist and suffer in a less desirable body and on a lower spiritual plane. He might even be reincarnated in the body of an animal or insect. However, if he kept on improving in his ability to subordinate the flesh and be absorbed in God, he might eventually attain release from the necessity of reincarnation and be poured back into the pool of undifferentiated Spirit from which his soul was originally drawn. This theory seems to the Theosophist to explain the otherwise inexplicable injustices of life. We suffer or live happily because of what we did in a previous incarnation. The difficulty that we cannot remember what we were or what we did which caused us to be what we are is met by the thought that we *are* actually given hints and intimations of previous lives if we only had the wit to put them together into a meaningful explanation. An Indian Christian recently received a letter from an outstanding Buddhist intellectual in Ceylon testifying to his belief that, from all sorts of subtle indications, his young son was the reincarnation of his grandfather! To those who do not share this belief, this seems the veriest nonsense; actually, it is beyond conclusive proof one way or the other.

There are many people who seem to derive inspiration, and a sort of guidance for the conduct of their affairs from the conception of a God who is supra-personal, impartial Justice. Through meditation and reflection the modern Theosophist attains a mystical experience in which the harsh and definite outlines of his own personality seem to be softened as he feels himself becoming absorbed in a peaceful, impersonal, spiritual Reality which underlies all the deceptive appearances of the physical life. Returning from these moments of absorption he believes that he sees the fret and agony of selfish, individual life in a new perspective. He feels called upon to express this vision for others in ways of beauty and significance. To be able in this life to be a channel for the personal exemplification of impersonal truth seems to him a sacred calling, just as ultimate identification with Impersonal Spirit seems to him the highest destiny. If he uses personal terms for God they should be understood as purely poetical and symbolic. It is peace of mind, rooted and grounded in basic spiritual Reality, that is the proper fruit of the divine wisdom, defined by the combination of two Greek words (*theos* for God, *sophos* for wisdom) as Theosophy.

Christian Scientists go beyond those who regard the physical as the *enemy* of the spiritual; they deny the *reality* of the physical, along with the existence of the corruptions and distortions of the physical known as disease, sin, evil and death. The foundation of this denial can be found in Mrs. Mary Baker Eddy's official interpretation of the Bible, known as *Science and Health:*

"First, God is all in all.
Second, God is good, good is mind.
Third, spirit being all, nothing is matter.
Fourth, life, God, omnipotent, good, deny death, evil, sin, disease—
Disease, sin, evil, death deny good, omnipotent, God, life." [8]

Matter is a "false concept of mortal mind." [9] This being the case, pain, sickness and suffering exist in the mind alone, are creatures of our inadequate and distorted mentalities, and have no actual existence in time and space. Sin seems to bedevil the human race because of an erroneous way of looking at things. The cure for sin as error is obviously to embrace the Truth. If one were able continually to be receptive to the Truth and nothing but the Truth, he would never experience pain, sickness or sin in his own person. He would be completely at one with God who is the Truth, and who does not acknowledge the reality of pain or sin. Death is unreal, also, because the immortal part of everyone makes the transition from this world to the next, and the errors of mortal mind which were responsible for the subjective imaginings known as physical discomfort and wrongdoing are immediately corrected, once a person "passes on" and has his spiritual eyes fully opened.

Mary Baker Eddy (1821–1910) was the founder of

Christian Science. She believed herself to be the revealer of the Truth for the modern world. She felt it was she who brought the Comforter whom Jesus foretold in the Fourth Gospel. The Comforter is actually the Science of Christianity which is the true contemporary interpretation of New Testament teaching, and is available to everyone who wishes to rid himself of the costly errors of distorted thought. Anyone, obviously, can derive great benefit from a study of the Bible, but the inner meaning of the message is far better understood if accompanied by a faithful reading of *Science and Health*.[10]

Mrs. Eddy was born in Bow, New Hampshire, the sixth child of a well-to-do farmer and his wife, both Congregationalists. In the 1820's, however, this meant that Mary was brought up on Calvinistic theology and she reacted violently against it. Her first husband was a contractor, who profited greatly from his ownership of slaves. After his death from yellow fever, Mary spent most of the money she inherited in freeing the slaves and educating her small son. She then married Dr. Patterson, a shiftless dentist with a wandering eye, who did her at least one good turn: he introduced her to Phineas P. Quimby, a healer who helped her tremendously and who sowed in her mind the seeds of what was to become Christian Science. Quimby had written, "Disease is false reasoning. False reasoning is sickness and death." Mary elaborated this idea, gave it metaphysical underpinnings, and so launched her new faith. She was then fortunate enough to meet and marry Asa Gilbert Eddy, who advised her on financial and practical matters, and saw to it that her new book, *Science and Health*, was protected by airtight copyright from being pirated. She lectured in Boston, inaugurated groups of followers and students, and enjoyed amazing success. She started a college and launched a newspaper, "The Christian Science Monitor," which has become one of the finest journals in the country. True to its founder, it still soft-pedals crime, scandal, illness, death and unsavory politics. Mary Baker Eddy exemplified the dynamic and radiant quality which her faith so often brought to people, and although frail herself, and practically snatched from the jaws of death by Mr. Quimby, she lived to be eighty-nine. Over six hundred and fifty churches in America alone acknowledge their allegiance to her tenets.

God, to the Scientist, is Divine Mind, and Mind is all that truly exists. The spirit of man was created by God, but matter is an illusion subject to disappear as Truth is more and more fully known. Man is essentially good as God is good; however, through the failure of mortal mind he does things which appear wrong; he experiences sensations which seem real to him, though they are illusory. Health comes when man is attuned to Truth; illness and disease are delusions which can be dissipated by prayer. Healing, therefore, must be religious, not secular; spiritual, not physical.

The Scientist accepts Jesus as divine but not as God; he was simply the son of God. His healings were not miracles, but merely demonstrations of the power of mind over matter. He is not to be thought of as one person of a trinity. The triune God consists of "life, truth and love," the "triple divine principle."[11] According to Mrs. Eddy, there could be no Incarnation, because flesh is unreal. There was no Cross, because Jesus was not really crucified. There was no Resurrection, because Jesus was at no time in the power of unreal death or matter. But he was supremely a healer; he healed solely by bringing the Truth to bear upon the errors of mortal mind. It is through faith in what he taught, as elaborated and explained in *Science and Health,* that salvation from the domination of false ideas may be gained.

Here again, God is not conceived as the personal being of the more traditional denominations, but rather as impersonal Truth, Mind, Spirit. He is not responsible for evil; evil seems to exist because man, though eternal and essentially spiritual, is fallible enough to allow his mortal mind the upper hand, and hence imagines that evil is real. The practical effect of this belief is, of course, helpful and invigorating to those who are inclined to be fretful, neurotic, doubtful, fearful. By disbelieving in pain and sin, the Scientist tries to rise above what seem to be the hideous realities of life for most people, and attains a happy outlook and a confident feeling of cooperation with the Divine Mind.

We have now examined, in the chronological order of their establishment in the form we now know them, the Mormons, Seventh-day Adventists, Spiritualists, Jehovah's Witnesses, Theosophists, and Christian Scientists. There is certainly no common denominator under all of these, except their deviation from evangelical Protestantism. Every one of these groups has adherents who are a credit to the human race; and yet each one uses the term God with a different meaning. Their Deities reveal themselves in different ways. Mormons look to the Book of Mormon to reveal the true significance of the Bible; Seventh-day Adventists follow Ellen Harmon White's interpretation of the Scriptures; Jehovah's Witnesses are guided by the commentaries of Charles T. Russell and Judge Rutherford; the Christian Scientists believe in the interpretation of the Gospel found in the writings of Mary Baker Eddy. All four of these groups claim to be rooted and grounded in the Word, but none will accept the results of the patient literary and historical criticism worked out by those theological scholars who have devoted their lives to a study of the Scriptures. For the Mormons, both matter and spirit have existed from eternity; for the Scientist, matter does not exist at all. For the Adventists, God is intensely personal; for the Scientists, God is impersonal Mind. The Mormons are almost tritheistic in their insistence on the distinctions within the personality of God; Jehovah's Witnesses are, to all intents and purposes, binitarian, since Jehovah and Jesus together are all the persons of the Godhead one needs; the Adventists claim to believe in the Trinity, conceived as most evangelical Protestants do; the Scientists are strongly monotheistic, but their God tends to be spoken of and worshipped as Impersonal Spirit, although apostrophized as Father-Mother-God; the God of Spiritualism seems a vague and shadowy background for the drama of the living and the dead, in which the living inherit an after-life simply because they are human and personal, and can have communication with those still on earth. The Deity for Theosophists is suprapersonal, essentially impersonal, the All-Soul, the undifferentiated Spirit-Essence in which all truly spiritual individuals will eventually lose their selfhood.

Yet all these groups use the word God. What does God himself think of the various approaches that are made to him, the various conceptions of his nature in the light of which people bow their heads in prayer? The superficial idea that all human beings can be divided into those who believe in God and those who do not breaks down when one examines the meaning of the word. One certainly knows agnostics who are more "religious" than some theists. Let us not try to smooth over the real differences among men; let us learn to understand them, know why they are there, and base our unity with our fellow men on grounds other than a mere semantic agreement.

CHAPTER 8

The God of the Righteous

"WHAT doth the Lord require of thee, but to do justly, to love mercy, and to walk humbly with thy God?" Thus Micah summarized the essence of Yahweh's demands upon men in the eighth century before Christ. God is just, merciful and holy; the only way to serve that kind of Deity is by being just and merciful and humble yourself. The character of God determines the kind of life he wishes man to lead. Conversely, it is the type of life man believes God wants him to lead that reveals better than anything else the kind of Deity he worships. Kali, for example, is thought of as a cruel goddess: that is, cruel to those who are not her devotees; therefore it is a religious duty for her worshippers to oppose and eliminate her enemies. The more "religious" a worshipper of Kali is, the more dangerous to the white man in certain parts of north India. Modern Hinduism regards this special devotion to the wife of Siva with disfavor; the cult is reportedly dying out. But in its heyday it was a striking illustration of the truth we are setting forth: the character of a god determines the morality esteemed among the devotees, and the practice of the devotees reflects the idea of the Deity's nature.

It is at this point that agnostic psychologists advance the notion that the religious man simply projects an idea of God into the sky of such a character as to satisfy his needs and to justify his behavior. For instance, Freud maintained that it was man's human desire for some sort of cosmic understanding that caused him to invent a Father in Heaven, and thus he has come to believe that the demands of his own super-ego within are a clue to the will of God above. Many apologists for Christianity dislike this line of reasoning intensely, although we notice that they often apply it to non-Christian religions while insisting that their own faith is differently based. They are fond of reminding us that because plural marriage was a traditional solution to the problem of the family in seventh-century Arabia, it was easy for Mohammed to fool himself into believing that God dictated his divine approval of the arrangement in the Koran. This is an extremely difficult matter on which to dogmatize. If anything comes to seem axiomatically right and socially beneficial in experience, a devout man will believe that God wills it; if anything seems to be a serious banc to society, a devout man will believe that God dislikes it. Micah may say that Yahweh desires man to "do justly"; but there will be a difference of opinion, at different periods in history, on what is justice. Our intelligence must play its part; tested experience obviously must be consulted in any determination of what is right and wrong. But the temptation to attribute to God the value-judgments we embrace is, of course, a dangerous one. As William Cole says, "Christians must always take care lest they confuse the word of man with the word of God."[1]

Samuel believed firmly that Yahweh wanted Saul to exterminate the Amalekites because they opposed Israel, and to slaughter their king Agag as well as all their domestic animals. When Saul, after massacring the people, saved the best of the flocks and also spared the ruler, Samuel was furious. He regretted that he had made Saul king; he "cried to the Lord all night." When he met Saul, he asked about the "bleating of the sheep" and the "lowing of the oxen" which he heard. Saul made the somewhat lame excuse that he fully intended to sacrifice these to the Lord. Samuel countered with the statement which, wrenched from its context, has always been a favorite text for sermons: "To obey is better than sacrifice."[2] It is possible to argue that, at that time, under those circumstances, Yahweh would have directed the annihilation of the Amalekites because they were "sinners" and stood in the way of Israel's fullest development. But it is also possible to argue that Samuel's passionate and bloodthirsty patriotism impelled him to attribute to God what was only his own consuming desire. However, we are in no position to be too patronizing towards what we may feel to be the limitations of Samuel's outlook. We are still discussing whether it was God's will or not for our war leaders, who were members of Christian Churches, to sanction retaliatory obliteration bombing, and the releasing of the atomic devices on Hiroshima and Nagasaki. At the time, these obvious evils were perpetrated in the conviction that they would help to save the human race from even more disastrous evils. I imagine we all have met people who are not convinced that our use of the A-bomb was contrary to the will of God; we have also known many who believe that, under the circumstances, it was the only thing to do, and hence was divinely approved. And there are still others who, deeply disturbed by the whole problem of man's incredible power to destroy, are not sure either way, and are more ready to pray for divine forgiveness than to claim divine sanction.

It is not only in spectacular matters such as these that we should be careful not to "confuse the word of man with the word of God." To "walk humbly" surely means to be vigilant against projecting our human value-judgments into the structure of the universe and calling them God's. At the same time, we must pray for deliverance from the complete futility of that relativism in which we are never able to feel that God has a definite will for us at all. Whatever our theory of revelation may be, a Christian does believe that God took the initiative in revealing his will in countless ways, but especially through the mouths of the prophets and life of his Son. I may be puzzled about many things, but as a Christian I should not be puzzled about my obligation to love God with my whole heart and soul and strength and mind, and my neighbor as myself. I will never be able to do this perfectly, but I will never be able to escape from the attempt; and, as long as I believe in the Father of our Lord Jesus Christ, I will never be able to hate or cheat or exploit my neighbor and claim I am doing God's will.

I should like now to have you examine with me some of the intricacies of this problem. In Dr. Moffatt's translation of Mark 9:32 we read, "They did not understand what he (Jesus) said, and they were afraid to ask him what he meant." In the Gospel this refers to our Lord's prediction of his death and resurrection; for us it might easily apply to the doing of his will. It is very difficult at times to know what Jesus would say or what God would desire, which, if we are Christians, is one and the same thing; we are puzzled, and we do often misunderstand. But sometimes our bewilderment is increased by our fear of asking God what he really means. When we take God consciously into spiritual partnership as we try to decide what is right and wrong, we often conclude that he asks far more of us than any easy-going impulses would demand. On the other hand, if we develop an unhealthily masochistic or puritanical attitude towards life, we may feel that God is more strict with us than would seem reasonable to freer souls. Mark Twain once said, "Many people are troubled about the scriptures which are . . . hard to understand. I am most troubled about those which I *can* understand!" I am sure we have had that experience when, for example, we have been tempted to dodge an unpleasant duty. Augustine's "love God and do as you please" seems like a welcome release from legalism until we suddenly realize that the deepest love of God may lead to a cross; and even the fact that this comes to be what we "please" does not always make it easier. And yet some unhealthy souls "please" to mortify the flesh and court martyrdom in a misguided conviction that God inevitably demands "sacrifice" of his children and the doing of what is unpleasant or painful.

The vagaries of the human mind in this realm are wondrous to behold. We sometimes run across a case where piety seems to be used as a perfume to kill the aroma of the unsavory. Albert Anastasia, shot to death in a New York barbershop by two mobsters, was widely reputed to have been behind one of the most notorious criminal outfits in our recent history: Murder, Incorporated. One of the investigating policemen, characterizing Anastasia's private life, reported him as being a singularly "devout" man. One wonders how long he had been "devout." Was he "devout" all through the period when he is said to have helped to engineer over fifty murders? Was he "devout" all the time he was master-minding some of the most lucrative rackets in greater New York? Does being "devout" mean more than going to Confession and being regular at Mass? What conception of religion would make it possible to be a pious gangster?

One hears of "religious" prostitutes in Paris who are regular in their attendance at church. One does not need to judge them in order to inquire by what spiritual rationalization they reconcile the service of God with the following of the "oldest profession." It is possible that they experience no more sense of contradiction than does any candid Christian who knows he is a sinner. "Love God and do what you please" has often been stretched to cover almost anything one finds it profitable to do. Of course, there does seem a difference between a "devout" prostitute and a "devout" mobster. The prostitute may not be seriously hurting anyone by what she does; the mobster may be pushing the sale of narcotics to minors.

But let us go to the other extreme. Almost twenty years ago a man died in this country who listed himself in *Who's Who* as a "reformer." He was a sincere, practicing Christian. He was a civic leader; he stood for honesty in public life. He was an ardent opponent of Fascism, Nazism and Communism. He was happily married, and generous with his money. He was largely instrumental in securing the passage of a New York City ordinance banning smoking from the subways, a law which even smokers approve. But this man believed that God wished human beings to restrict themselves to "natural" food and drink, and therefore he conducted a life-time campaign against not only liquor but tea, coffee and manufactured soft drinks. One of his favorite sayings was, "When a deer in the forest fastness wishes to quench its thirst, it seeks not a brew but crystal water from natural brooks." He was against the chocolate ice-cream soda. He was an unalterable opponent of the lollypop. He did not believe that women should use cosmetics, and he was against any artificial constriction of any part of the female figure. He had courage: he would often step up to a person smoking illegally on a subway platform, take the cigarette out of his mouth, throw it down and stamp it out, in spite of protests and an occasional punch in the nose. To him the use of tobacco was against the will of God anyway, but especially where it befouled the air so that non-smokers suffered. It was very difficult for this gentleman to go out to dinner where alcohol and tobacco were served and keep his own counsel. His social reputation was that of a crank and a bore; yet he was a "good" man.

Dr. John Harvey Kellogg was somewhat the same type. He had strong convictions, both moral and medical, against the use of not only tobacco, liquor, tea, and coffee, but also of meat. He was always attempting to concoct vegetarian foods which would be as appetizing as those indulged in by meat-eaters. In 1895, he devised wheat flakes, but he really hit the jack-pot in 1902 when he invented corn flakes. He believed firmly that God approved his crusade. His Deity was strict when it came to the personal habits of the human race. Rigid discipline in matters of diet, sex, personal honesty and language was the only godly regime. It was almost a matter of his developing a new legalism for the ordering of the truly Christian life. Although most conservative Protestants in the decades immediately preceding and following the turn of the century would not have gone as far as Dr. Kellogg, especially in his vegetarianism, thousands felt the way he did about tobacco and liquor, which were so often associated in the minds of the pious with careless, not to say "loose," living.

I was brought up in a conservative Baptist home in Canada, and my father was an ardent campaigner against smoking and drinking, especially the latter. The saloons of

Toronto before World War I were notorious. The liquor lobbies in the Canadian Parliament, as well as in Congress and in the State Legislatures across the border, were powerful and unscrupulous. Regulations carefully drawn were continually broken. Police departments were bribed to look the other way when violations were committed. Saloons were often concentrated near factories so that when the workers received their pay on Saturday afternoons they would run the gauntlet of opportunities to "relax" before the Sabbath. Many employees arrived home in fine spirits but minus a considerable portion of their weekly wages. The liquor interests were also mixed up with vice. It seemed logical for consecrated Christians to renounce drink and denounce its manufacturers and vendors. If to be a Christian was to live a life of love towards God and neighbor, and if the whole beverage alcohol business seemed set to defy God and ruin one's neighbor, how could a follower of Jesus have any part in it?

Furthermore, money was considered a sacred trust; each Christian was a steward for God. How could one justify spending hard-earned money on alcohol, which endangered the individual and corrupted society, when so many good causes cried out for support? This feeling about the importance of stewardship applied also to ostentation and extravagance as well as to gambling. In our home, these were all considered wrong, although drinking was especially blameworthy, as it was not only expensive but dangerous. Those who believed in moderation rather than teetotalism used to point out that Jesus drank wine in his day. This, however, seemed irrelevant to the godly in that particular period. In first-century Palestine there was no highly organized industry designed to promote sales of intoxicants by bribing authority and breaking the law. My parents' feeling, I remember, was that if Jesus walked the earth in America during the early nineteen hundreds, he too would have taken his stand for total abstinence, if not for prohibition.

The situation is somewhat changed today. We have had prohibition and its by-products were worse than the evils it intended to eliminate. Rightly or wrongly, the use of beverage alcohol in moderation does not seem inconsistent with devotion to Christ and his cause for an increasing number of intelligent Protestants. It never has seemed inconsistent to Rome, nor does it to the majority of those groups represented in the World Council of Churches. As the feeling grows that moralism does not represent true Christianity, the reaction against sumptuary legislation and the criticism of personal habits becomes stronger. Modern Christians may give up smoking as it becomes clearer that its physical effects are more dangerous than formerly thought. They give up drinking if they find that its effect on them is harmful. They diet if they feel they are overweight. But they are not nearly so inclined as were their grandfathers to make a moral, not to say theological, issue out of matters like these. If a person has accepted God in Christ he becomes a new creature who is given guidance and strength to show forth Christian love in his life. He takes no Pharisaical credit for forswearing certain doubtful personal habits, nor does he feel guilty if he goes to a party and takes a drink. What God demands of him is not to be "good," but to be good for something; not to be "righteous" but to be intelligently sensitive to the needs of others. If the foregoing describes a perceptible shift in the attitude of many devoted people, then it also describes a subtle change in what is believed to be God's attitude towards his children.

The present-day Protestant is not inclined to make light of sin, or treat it as mere maladjustment. He recognizes that he is a child of God but also a sinner. Sin is essentially *estrangement*, of man from God and of man from man. Tillich maintains that *anxiety* is the root of the trouble: anxiety about the temporary character of our earthly existence, anxiety about the apparent meaninglessness of our lives, anxiety over our guilty condition. We do not wish to face the fact of death; we assert our own self-centered importance as somehow establishing our meaningfulness; we try to fool ourselves into believing that we are not so bad after all. And all the time we need to accept God, who promises us life everlasting, who convinces us of our essential sonship and therefore as having eternal significance, and who forgives us so that our guilt does not need to continue weighing us down. A *legal* system is naturally concerned about *sins* and their punishment or remission; a *religious* gospel is concerned about *sin* and its forgiveness in restoration and reconciliation.

The Catholic penchant for making pronouncements on matters of manners and morals is much more evident than in contemporary Protestantism, except for the more conservative sects. One rarely hears a sermon by a Congregationalist attempting to define the difference between a mild and a serious sin where personal habits are concerned. Protestant preaching is more apt to set forth the nature of the Christian's obligation as one who is committed to love God and his neighbor, hoping that the individual will decide what is right and wrong for him. I know of few preachers or writers who would care to be specific about the number of daily packs of cigarettes consumed which would make smoking a sin.

And yet the Very Reverend Francis J. Connell, dean of

the School of Sacred Theology at the Catholic University in Washington, recently considered the subject of cigarette smoking in Notre Dame's *Ave Maria* magazine. He came to the conclusion that *moderate* smoking is not a sin, but that *immoderate* smoking is, especially now that science seems convinced of its connection with certain serious ailments. Even immoderate smoking for very healthy men might be only a *venial* sin, but for those who may be affected adversely in mental, physical, or spiritual well-being three packs a day may constitute a *mortal* sin.

The Italian Jesuit theologian, Armando Guidetti, maintains that it is a sin to engage in eating or drinking competitions where the one who consumes the most is the winner. He also declares it is a sin for a woman to diet to the point where she endangers her health. Whereas there is no objection to moderate social drinking, drunkenness is listed among mortal sins; partial drunkenness, involving a serious befuddling of the mind, is labelled a venial sin. All these sins should be confessed, and penance should be done for them.

Santa Fe's Archbishop Edwin V. Byrne warns the 70,000 parochial school-children under his care about the sinfulness of what he calls "pagan" practices: "going steady," "keeping steady company," "necking and kissing," even "handholding" and the "shared ice-cream soda." [3]

In November, 1957, the late Pope Pius XII outlined a code for fashion designers to clarify the Vatican's stand on what is permissible in the realm of *haute couture*. Much of the code makes perfectly good sense for any Christian. The Holy Father warned against the "indiscriminate provocation" of some styles, and hinted at his official displeasure concerning Bikini bathing-suits and plunging necklines. On the other hand, he did not advocate unbecoming or puritanical adornment for young women, but dress which exhibits youthful charm without involving partial nudity or exhibitionism. The Church does not condemn fashion, or disapprove of mere ornamentation. Drawing the line between what is risqué or sinful and what is permissible is very difficult, the Pontiff agreed, but the starting-point should be in the intention of the designers and wearers. Moving-picture actresses have a special responsibility to set a good example to the young in this regard, he maintained.

The significance of all this lies not in the details, but in the idea that the ordinary Catholic should have the guidance of the Church on moral matters, both those which are obvious and those which are debatable. I attended classes, several years ago, for three consecutive days in a parochial high school. I was very much interested to see what wide latitude was given by the teachers to the pupils in the discussion of ethical questions. No attempt was made to suppress any point of view, no matter how far it seemed to deviate from the official Catholic position. However, five minutes before the end of each class, the teaching "brother" who was in charge would say, "It has been very stimulating to hear the various opinions which have been expressed. I shall now try to make quite clear to you what the Church teaches on this subject." He would then proceed to explain the matter in terms of specific quotations from Thomas Aquinas or some other medieval scholar, or from an encyclical, or from the Bible as interpreted by the Church. There could be no possible doubt in any student's mind as to what the Catholic teaching was or what every member of the school's faculty believed. Officially, the instructors presented a united front. For city children, caught up in the confusions of the modern world and blown about by various winds of doctrine, all this must have induced a welcome sense of security.

The picture of God implied in Catholic practice is of a Divine Ruler who works through his Church and his vicar on earth to set certain definite standards for the behavior of his children: standards which will guard them against the onslaughts of a secular and pagan world. He is not overly grim or austere, although he may sometimes seem so. He is often conceived as far more tolerant than the God of conservative Protestantism. Actually, some Protestant chaplains in the war were taken aback at the way the Catholic chaplains got "next" to the G. I.'s by drinking with them and fraternizing with them as they gambled or swapped stories. Furthermore, Catholics think there are many intermediaries, especially the Virgin and the saints, who plead for weak mortals before the throne of the Most High, and the Church is careful to instruct the faithful about the concrete means by which, through confession and penance, sins can be forgiven and the burdened conscience relieved. For many souls, this is more reassuring than the more theologically sophisticated message of neo-orthodoxy, or the more strait-laced moral injunctions of the fundamentalist sects.

As one further example of the contrast, let us look at the attitude of conservative Protestantism and of Roman Catholicism towards gambling. A classic Protestant definition is as follows: "Gambling occurs when, as the result of a bet, property is transferred from one to another upon the occurrence of an event which, to the two parties to the bet, was a matter of complete chance, or as nearly so as their adjustment of conditions could make it." [4] Gambling, in the volume from which this definition comes, is adjudged morally wrong for the following reasons: Property represents labor; it stands for a man's life-blood. The possession of property is a sober responsibility, which should be used for the highest good of the owner, the benefit of the public, and the glory of God. The sound use of reason should guide any transfer of property; gambling deliberately eliminates or minimizes the use of reason in connection with a transfer of property. Gambling is wrong because it is a surrender to chance of acts which should be controlled by reason alone, and therefore it operates outside the moral law. The only motive for gambling is the desire to get something for nothing through chance. This motive should surely be beneath the serious consideration of a consecrated Christian. It is a frivolous risking of what represents someone's labor for the sake of an unearned reward.

If this sounds a bit ponderously puritanical, it is well to remember that it is a somewhat labored attempt to find plausible reasons for a serious moralist's antipathy towards a practice which, though associated with a carefree sporting impulse, actually has been the downfall of many an individual. A wager between two men who can afford to lose has no particular significance one way or the other; serious gambling by those who cannot afford to lose can become a corrosive vice which eats away the determination to earn a livelihood by honest toil. A man who has surrendered himself to God to be used for noble purposes cannot afford to engage in this practice. It is one thing to bet on a golf game with the loser paying for the caddy; it is another and a different thing to risk a fortune on the turn of a card or the speed of a horse. Most Protestant moralists condemn gambling as an un-Christian pastime, even in its milder forms.

The Roman Church does not share this attitude. According to Catholic thinkers moderate gambling is a relatively harmless pursuit, as is the temperate use of beverage alcohol. Just because some people ruin themselves by betting and "booze" is no reason for condemning them outright. These things give many people much innocent pleasure. The Church, of course, capitalizes on the mild excitement of Bingo to swell the holy coffers, a practice seriously frowned on by Methodists, Baptists and Presbyterians.

According to the leading sports writer of the *New York Herald Tribune,* the pastor of St. Peter's Catholic Church at Saratoga keeps an eye on how well the pari-mutuel machines are patronized, and suggests, on a Sunday morning following a particularly active Saturday, that successful betters can assist the work of the Lord by dropping their earnings in the collection baskets. This same reporter, Red Smith, tells of hearing a sermon by a fine-looking young priest at Edgartown on Martha's Vineyard who was trying to raise some money for foreign missions. In the course of his sermon he said, "My father ran a trolley car in Boston and I don't have to tell you things weren't easy for him financially. One day two Sisters of Charity got on his car, and when they were about to get off he handed each one a dollar.

" 'Sisters,' he told them, 'I'd like you to take this, please, and use it for whatever purpose you think best.'

"This was true charity, because $2.00 meant a great deal to my father, but this was a gift from the heart. It was charity that must be rewarded, and that same afternoon—that very afternoon—my father hit the daily double at Suffolk, and he got plenty." [5]

It would be hard to imagine an incident like that being used in a sermon in a Methodist Church in the Middle West, even granting that the preacher's father had a comparable experience! The Roman Church, of course, frowns upon the ruinous gambling in which many people engage, a pastime which involves the risk of losing what should go for the support of the family; but God is not thought of as frowning upon modest wagers, bets and lotteries. About many matters there is a somewhat latitudinarian tolerance in the Roman view which contrasts sharply with that of Reformed moralists.

Of course, it sometimes works the other way. The Vatican takes a strong stand against birth control where Protestantism either refuses to legislate, or tolerates, or even recommends. This strong feeling against interfering with the natural results of intercourse is interpreted by the unsympathetic as motivated by a simple desire for more Catholics. But the problem is surely more complicated than that. The Church is afraid that the widespread use of contraceptives will not only limit the size of families, but also encourage pre-marital and extra-marital license; this fear seems to be borne out by recent studies. On the other hand, some priests quietly tolerate the use of birth-control as but a venial sin for the urban poor living in crowded conditions. Large families were an economic asset in agricultural countries; now large families are often a terrific economic liability, and a child in a family of four gets many opportunities for health, attention and individual development which that same child would not get in a family of ten. Even the Church sometimes tempers the wind to the shorn lamb; but officially the Vatican has spoken, and that is that.

The view of God's will here implied is a logical one, granted the premises. It is through the Church that the continuing authority of Christ is maintained. The Church, in solemn conclave, can formulate new doctrines for the meeting of new conditions in an authoritative way well nigh impossible for a Protestant denomination. What Rome sacrifices in freedom she feels she more than makes up in security. God is not considered the intimate spiritual companion of every Christian *apart from* the Church's dogma and structure. The hierarchy was developed through the ages; the hierarchy continues to rule. No "grass-roots" democracy is desirable when tradition, continuity, apostolic succession, spiritual authority are concerned.

Ernest Jones, the biographer of Freud, summarizes one central conclusion reached by the psychoanalytic studies of religion in these words: "The religious life represents a dramatization on a cosmic scale of the emotions, fears, and longings which arose in the child's relations to his parents." [6] This provocative notion has by now become almost a cliché. There is just enough truth in it, as applied to some phenomena, to tempt the unwary into making it cover too much. It does not explain fully what Coe called "the religion of the mature mind." It does not explain the subtleties of Tillich's theology, or the faith of a sophisticated Catholic. But it does point up the way in which childhood experiences can condition one's evaluation of what he believes God's value-judgments to be. Fortunately for all of us, these do not stay put. The mature person keeps changing. He becomes much less sensitive to certain promptings of conscience which bothered him as a child, and his conscience develops scruples which never would have crossed his mind as a youngster. If he is a religious person, his view of God's desires for him change accordingly. And when he takes the Freudian view of religion into account he is apt to say, "Certainly there is a lot of truth in it, especially when one considers how the conscience is formed by early experiences in the family." This does not mean that he has to remain at the emotional level of childhood. He can learn to grow, to become more objective, to suspect his own motivations, to transcend his own childish evaluations of things. His view of God's will changes and evolves as he comes to see more and learn more and read more and suffer more. Let me illustrate this from my own experience, which, I imagine, will prove to be the experience of many of those who read these words.

I was brought up in a strictly sabbatarian household. In Toronto in the first decade of the century, street-cars did not run on the Sabbath, all places of amusement were closed, no public games like football or baseball were played. At home, Sunday was a day different from all the others: no secular music was heard, no games were played. One went to Sunday-school and church. One visited with friends. Family dinners were held. No one worked on the Sabbath, except the cook, and she always finished up her labors by two in the afternoon.

My mother died when I was eleven, my father when I was thirteen, and I was adopted into an older sister's family. My brother-in-law had been brought up to "remember the Sabbath Day to keep it holy," but in my new home, as long as the children went to Sunday-school and church, we could read what we liked, play what games we fancied, even sing popular songs around the piano or have a "jam session." But we did *not* go to the movies on Sunday, and there were no theaters operating that day, so we did observe a few of the prohibitions laid down by those of the generation gone by.

Once, while I was on a trip with a college dramatic troupe, I happened to be in a strange mid-western city over the weekend. We had played a show on Saturday, we were to move on to another town on Monday, but we were resting up at the local hotel on the Sabbath. I went to church in the morning, and then discovered that a legitimate theater, right across the street from where we were staying, was having a matinée and an evening performance of a play I very much wanted to see. I had never been to the theater on Sunday. At lunch along with several of my classmates in the troupe, I decided that it would be fun to attend the matinée. I admit that it was with mixed feelings that I paid my money and took my seat. I enjoyed the play, except for the fact that I felt slightly uncomfortable whenever I realized just what day it was. My father's conditioning was still with me. As a boy I would undoubtedly have interpreted the voice of conscience about "breaking the Sabbath" as the voice of God. On the other hand, my brother-in-law, now *in loco parentis* to me, had imposed no such stringent legalism on his family as my father had done. So, under the circumstances, my conscience bothered me a little, but not enough to disturb me inordinately. I was conscious that God might feel mildly disapproving of what I was doing. As I left the theater, I felt the need for confession; so in a light-hearted letter which had a few serious undertones, I wrote to my sister and her husband making a clean breast of my violation of the family taboo, and asking for absolution. I got an amusing letter back, the burden of which was that the "Sabbath was made for man and not man for the Sabbath," and that the old-fashioned rules of conservative Protestantism were not necessarily the only guides for those who wished to keep the Sabbath holy. Experience has since taught me much about the value of Sunday. I still believe that I should attend a service, to join with others in the worship of God, to identify myself with the Church visible. But if something exceptional intervenes, or work that must be done by Monday piles up frighteningly, I no longer feel uncomfortable about how I use the Sabbath. I am sure many Christians have had similar experiences concerning this matter as well as others.

One might say that God, originally though unconsciously identified with the rules laid down by parents, comes to be thought of as a Being with whom one has communion, and not merely as a strict Task-master forever concerned with childhood *mores*. In a home, a skillful parent becomes progressively less of a moralist and more of a companion. The same thing can happen with one's view of God. If it does, then the individual is beginning to achieve a mature religion; and there is no metaphysical reason for insisting that just because one's developing sense of the Divine parallels his developing emotional maturity that the idea of God is a mere projection or "dramatization on a cosmic plane" of his family experiences. One's concept of God as a Personal Father, one's image of the Father of our Lord Jesus Christ, may be as near to the working truth about the ultimate Power behind everything as the human mind can grasp; it may very well be that it takes the experience of self-understanding and progressive independence of emotional domination by the family to enable anyone to form a truly Christian concept of God. At this point, man's imaginative projection of the divine idea must be continually enriched by mature experience. One never becomes completely mature; one never achieves a completely satisfying idea of God. But there is no reason to believe that we are so enclosed within our own selfhood that what begins as a "projection" has no reality as an object. If one pushes this thought to its logical conclusion, he may end up as a solipsist; and too many things "come" to us from outside, from "deep down" within, from the past, from "beyond," to permit the average man to believe that he is cut off from reality except as he projects the phantoms of his mind onto a psychic screen and takes this endogenic construction as reality.

Sometimes we have the experience of becoming *more* conscientious about something than we ever could have been when we were young. The development of scientific integrity undoubtedly falls in this classification. In my own case, one other personal illustration will suffice. As a theological student I was acting as an assistant in a church in New York City which ministered to a large number of impoverished families on the Upper East Side. I had the sometimes grim task of making pastoral calls on families living in many old-fashioned, illegal "dumb-bell" tenements. In apartments in these buildings, the living room was at the front on the street, and the kitchen at the back on the areaway. They were the only two rooms which had windows; the two rooms in between were like the central post of a dumb-bell, with no light from outside except that which came through the doors from either the living room or the kitchen. In one home it was my duty to visit, two of the children slept in the first windowless room, two more in the second room, also windowless, and the father and mother in the kitchen. There was only one bed for every two human beings. One day one of the children became ill; the doctor was called too late; in a few days the child died in bed with her sister beside her. During the next week, the sister also died. I assisted at both funerals.

Poverty, squalor, and ignorance here went hand in hand. I happened to be rather well-heeled at the time. For years I had studied the extremes of wealth and poverty in the world, but it had never come home to me as vitally as during that period when I would work all day in the slums, and then retire to a first-rate restaurant and enjoy a good dinner, with my check paid by money I had inherited from my father, who died ten years before. Suddenly I became somewhat morbidly sensitive about my spending. Along with several others at the seminary, I decided to live a life of voluntary poverty. It never went very deep or lasted very long, but even today I think twice before spending money frivolously, knowing how much a few dollars mean, here and especially abroad, to people who struggle and struggle and never do make ends meet. This is a case where first-hand experience produced a sensitizing of the conscience in a realm where no particular issue was seen before. It was easy for me to imagine that God was disturbed about the distribution of wealth on earth. For a time I was a Socialist and voted for Norman Thomas; this did not sit particularly well with my brother-in-law and surely would have made my father turn over in his grave. But I believe it illustrates my point: our view of God's will for us is and must always be deeply affected by our experience in trying to live up to the moral vision we already have. For one of my classmates at the theological seminary, this meant a call to poverty with such dramatic results that he had to give up his graduate studies to "identify himself" completely with the most underprivileged group in our society. For another of my classmates, this meant the acceptance of a call to a wealthy church with the idea of doing missionary work for the social gospel. With me it meant accepting a position in Egypt where the difference between rich and poor was even greater than in the United States in the twenties.

No matter what people claim, our idea of God is bound to be affected by our social experience. All psychologists understand the prevalence of rationalization in our thinking. To them this means primarily that we try to find reasons which justify to our superego doing what we wish to do. But there are two other possible meanings to the word: it is used in economics to describe the process of "making reasonable" or "subjecting to reason" those aspects of our commercial life which otherwise would be carried on without reference to logic. It can also be used as we seek to "make reasonable" to ourselves the nature of the power behind the universe in the light of those values we feel to be the highest in our experience, and therefore something which the ultimate power must care for too. In this sense, and individual's maturing style of life, with increasingly broad sympathies and increasingly deep insights, must affect his view of God's hopes for humanity, and must contribute to his "rationalization" of religion.

If this is true of individuals like Francis of Assisi, who renounced a life of privilege for a life of happy poverty and in the process felt the joy of sharing what he believed was his Master's experience on earth, it is also true for racial and cultural development. Israel started with a God conceived as tribal enjoining benevolence towards Israelites and enmity to all others; Israel began with little consideration for women as people, and no consideration at all for slaves as human beings; Israel began with moral duties conceived as obedience to external conformity. And this same Israel, by the time a thousand years had gone by, had produced prophets who believed that Yahweh was the God of *all* the nations, that women and slaves were to be treated as children of the Most High, and that obedience to the will of the Deity was a matter of catching his spirit rather than obeying his code. The character of God changed as the experience of men broadened and deepened; and God could not teach them faster than they could learn. Here it is not a matter of choice between Freud and the Apostle Paul; God's revelation is primary, but man's capacity for the acceptance and understanding of revelation seems to come only as he is tested and twisted and shocked and humbled by life. Then does his imagination project the image which later thinkers evaluate as truer than any more primitive conceptions. And God's will, once conceived as bent on the destruction of Agag, king of the Amalekites, may be, in our day, thought of as bent upon the redemption of all men, even Communists!

In some matters it seems to a conscientious Christian easy to tell what is right and wrong, what God approves or disapproves. In other matters it seems extraordinarily difficult. One can place his moral decisions on a scale ranging from those where the right is obvious to those where the right is almost impossible to know. At one end could be found choices involving simple honesty, decency, thoughtfulness, kindness, living up to one's word, meeting one's obligations, fulfilling one's promises. In many of these matters, things decide themselves once a moment's serious thought is given to them. If one "takes it to the Lord in prayer," he does not decide to lie out of a difficult responsibility in favor of selfish indulgence. He may do so after a couple of drinks, or under the influence of an irresponsible crowd, but he probably kicks himself around the block afterwards. It sometimes seems a bit grandiose to bring God into the making of decisions which should be self-evident. There is an advantage in doing the effective, the sensible, the sporting thing just because it is what the objective situation calls for, without reference to an Ultimate Being at all. Harry Emerson Fosdick preached a famous sermon in the thirties entitled, "Six Ways to Tell Right from Wrong." He suggested that "if a man is sincerely perplexed about a question of right and wrong, he might well submit it to" the tests of common sense, sportsmanship, what his best self would sanction, how he would feel if his action were known to everyone, what the person he most admires would counsel, and where the contemplated behavior would lead. These are not rules; these are tests to be applied intelligently. One can easily believe that, for the most part, decisions made in their light would receive God's approval. There would still be differences of opinion on what is sensible, what is truly sportsmanlike, and the rest; there would still be many an interior dialogue necessary before one could be sure. But on the whole, choices made in these ways would be right.

I am one of those peculiar people who believe that a certain amount of neatness and orderliness is a moral obligation. I cringe when riding behind a sedan whose occupants throw banana-skins and waxed paper out of the windows to mess up the roadside. I believe that the Lord prefers unlittered landscapes to littered, but I also know that some of the finest Christians are not as fussy as I about these matters; and I admit that the whole world could be kept neat as a pin and still be the Kingdom of the Devil rather than of God: look at Hitler's Berlin. A perspicuous article in *The Christian Century* contains these sentences: "My ten-year-old son has an unfortunate habit of leaving his pajamas in the middle of the bedroom floor in the morning. Is it necessary that I point out that Jesus Christ would have picked up his own pajamas? There is certainly no direct scriptural warrant for such a midrash." There are many things that it is "right" to do without making an elaborate theological issue out of them.

I once moved a piano out from the wall of a private home, a piano on which I was to play the hymns for a small prayer-meeting. It was quite obvious that no one had swept under that piano for days. Afterwards the hostess was complaining to her husband about the way I moved her furniture around, and why she was embarrassed, when her little daughter said, "But Mummy, God sees under the piano."

It is dangerous to link up all moral decisions to theology in order to enforce them. Once a boy I know returned home from boarding-school on the afternoon of a big high-school dance, where all his friends of the year before could be found, and where plans could be made for the vacation. He announced this to his parents before dinner, and they informed him that since his Uncle Ben from California was arriving soon to visit he had better give up his idea of attending the party in favor of sitting at home with the family and his relative. He protested; so the father said, "All right, son, you go up into your room and pray; and if the Lord says it is all right for you to go dancing rather than visit with your uncle, who so seldom is able to come East, I will abide by the decision." The boy looked his father in the eye and said, "O.K., Dad, you win." I have often wondered why the lad could not have visited with his uncle until nine or so, and then attended the party. I think I would have admired the boy if he had gone upstairs and returned with a divine sanction for dining at home and then joining his friends. It is possible to argue that God does not care to be used in this way as a club to enforce family discipline.

But we all know of many decisions for which even prayer and profound thought do not yield a clear answer. We are caught in the relativities of society, and it is the part of wisdom to be very humble about the righteousness of our compromises. I have friends who are sure that it is wicked to spend money on liquor to provide entertainment for one's dinner guests; I do not believe it is easy to know this for sure. I have friends who believe that we, as Christian citizens, should work for unilateral disarmament, whether Russia continues to arm and resist international inspection or not; I find this hard to believe, and yet no one can be happy about the necessity of our staying armed to the teeth. I cannot be cocksure about the righteousness of the many political judgments one is called upon to make. I cannot believe that God is a Socialist any more than that he sanctions nothing completely but *laissez-faire* capitalism.

One thing we can be sure of: If we love our neighbor and earnestly strive to do what is right, we can trust that God will understand our involvement in the ambiguities of history, and will forgive us for our mistakes as we strive earnestly to do his will. And as we become more intelligently ethical we should also become more theologically mature; though we necessarily remain agnostics in many matters, we should come to have a clearer understanding of what it means to serve the Lord.

CHAPTER 9

The God of Hymn and Song

WHEN we come to examine the conception of God in the hymns of the Christian Church, we are confronted by a rather unusual fact: a great many people who sing hymns pay very little attention to the words, and therefore are not conscious of what sentiments they are expressing, or what theology they are affirming. Quite frequently I have used, as a prayer following the sermon, this quatrain:

> "I ask no dream, no prophet ecstasies;
> No sudden rending of the veil of clay;
> No angel visitant, no opening skies;
> But take the dimness of my soul away."

Scores of people have come up to me to ask where they could find that piece of poetry! They had sung "Spirit of God, descend upon my heart" a hundred times, but had paid so little heed to the words that they could not recognize one stanza when divorced from the music and the rest of the hymn. The tune to which the words are most frequently sung is a late nineteenth-century melody entitled *Morecambe* by Frederick C. Atkinson, which is looked upon with disfavor by musicians who dislike the sentimentality of this and many other hymn tunes of the period. In one of the newer and more fastidious hymnals, the words are set to Michael Wise's *Congleton,* a seventeenth-century melody with no regular rhythm, very much in the plain-song idiom, which probably will never become popular with the average Protestant congregation.

The poem itself is a simple prayer for power and light. The theology is theistic, though otherwise vague, and not particularly or distinctively Christian. But most people with whom I have talked are not so much impressed by the words as beguiled by the immediate singability of the tune *Morecambe,* which can be picked up after one hearing, and which insinuates itself into the system almost too easily and sweetly. They do not consider what the words say and mean. The Episcopal *Hymnal* omits the hymn entirely, possibly because it is not especially Christian. I am using this merely as an illustration of the common Protestant practice of singing hymns with little or no conscious attention to the words.

I remember when I first read "Holy, Holy, Holy" without the accompanying tune, *Nicaea.* I had never thought about the picture of the saints adoring God by "casting down their golden crowns around the glassy sea." Of course, this is figurative, and I recognize it as such, but I had sung the phrase for twenty years or more before that rather astonishing picture was suggested to my mind's eye. Whatever else one can say about the devotional poetry we call hymns, we can be sure that the writers did not wish their work to be taken lightly or cavalierly. Furthermore, if the words do actually, whether figuratively or not, represent the prayer and praise one would voice himself in different and possibly more prosaic words, hymns can be one of the most satisfying forms of religious expression. One does not have to believe in the literal existence of devils to sing "A mighty fortress is our God" as long as he believes that "God's truth abideth still" and that "His kingdom is forever." One does not have to believe in angels in order to sing "God, that madest earth and heaven," or in a physical Second Coming to sing "Rise, my soul." And there may be times when one can sing a splendid tune as an act of devotion even if the words express sentiments totally foreign to his convictions. But this is unsatisfactory; hymns were meant to be prayers, and should be sincere; it should be possible to take their poetic imagery *seriously* if not *literally*.

Unitarians rewrite some evangelical hymns in order that they may sing them with sincerity; they reduce the extreme trinitarianism to a simple theism. Some contemporary trinitarians, who feel uncomfortable about expressing themselves in terms of the "blood of the Lamb" and propitiatory atonement, will omit certain hymns entirely from the collections they edit. Some hymns will seem objectionable to editors because of their words, and others because of their music. In selecting appropriate hymns for services one may come to the conclusion that only those should be used where *both* the words and the music are acceptable. In a local church this might mean that the congregation would use a smaller number of hymns during the year. It might, however, encourage the learning of some strong, new hymns, such as "God of grace and God of glory" by Harry Emerson Fosdick, as well as the recovery of some fine ancient ones, such as "Be thou my vision," set to the grand old Irish tune *Slane*.

This process of editing, selection, rejection, creation, and re-discovery in hymnology has been going on for a long time, finally producing such outstanding collections as the *Hymnal for Colleges and Schools,* edited by E. Harold

Geer. This is a book specially designed for educational institutions where liberal evangelical Christianity goes hand in hand with high standards of literary criticism and musical taste. Here we find no "Jesus calls us o'er the tumult," set either to *Galilee* with its barber-shop harmony or to *Brocklesbury* with its undistinguished melody, no "Onward, Christian soldiers," no "Tell me the old, old story," no "Rock of ages," no "Work for the night is coming." But we do find such effective hymns as "Immortal, invisible" to *St. Denio,* "Awake my soul, and with the sun" to *Tallis Canon,* "Wake, awake, for night is flying" to Bach's harmonization of *Wachet Auf,* and "Praise the Lord, ye heavens adore him" to *Hyfrydol.* The average church congregation might not be happy in the somewhat rarefied atmosphere of this hymnal; but to change the figure (!) it does represent a bold flag nailed to a high mast in the interests of exacting standards.

Some acceptable words to lilting popular tunes, such as "Jesus calls us o'er the tumult," should be reset to better music. New hymns, both words and music, should be written. What is chiefly desirable at the moment, however, is the discovery and use of some of the twentieth-century hymns such as are found in the 1940 edition of the Protestant Episcopal *Hymnal,* and the rediscovery and use of the translations of Latin hymns, set to fine old melodies, such as have been collected in *Hymnal for Colleges and Schools.*[1] Whatever is done, the motive must be to glorify God, and worship him with dignity and beauty. It may be that one of the finest things that could happen to a church would be the initiation of a serious study of the poetry, theology and music of our Christian tradition, beginning with hymnology and proceeding to anthems, oratorios, masses and cantatas. We might find that the encouragement of worshippers to think hard about the words they sing might do much for the richness of their devotional life and the strengthening of their theology.

I remember how, in Oxford as a student, I was led to rededicate myself to God's work by the singing, one day in chapel, of John Keble's simple hymn, "New every morning is the love," which ends with the couplet, "and help us, this and every day, to live more nearly as we pray." I remember as a boy being very much disturbed by the phrase "where every prospect pleases, and only man is vile" in "From Greenland's icy mountains" (the stanza containing that phrase has been eliminated from most hymnals). I remember falling in love permanently with the music of Johann Sebastian Bach when introduced to his harmonization of Hassler's *Herzlich Tut Mich Verlangen* ("O Sacred head, now wounded"), and his arrangement of "Jesu, thou joy of man's desiring." I remember being intrigued by the notion behind Cowper's lines, "God moves in a mysterious way his wonders to perform," and being deeply impressed by the marriage of Haydn's melody and Addison's poem in "The spacious firmament on high." At the tender age of ten I was taken by my father to a Chapman-Alexander revival in Toronto, where I heard four thousand people sing, "O that will be glory for me"; as I look back on it I remember how fervently I believed that the sight of Jesus' face in heaven would be "glory" for anyone. That was also during the period in my life when we put our pennies through a slot in a box in Sunday School to the stirring four-four rhythm of "Hear the pennies dropping, listen how they fall; every one for Jesus, he will get them all." I was brought up in a church where poetry and doggerel, good theology and bad, noble melodies and sentimental tunes were all mixed up uncritically in a religious mélange of fundamentalist doctrine and intra-mundane asceticism. Sometimes the hymns and prayers were better than the dogma; often the music was far below the standard of what we heard in the concert-hall. But it was after I became conscious of what was being sung and celebrated in song and anthem that I began to realize how very important it is to offer to God our *best;* I came to feel that, for the worship of the Power behind the Universe, the ultimate ground of Existence, the God and Father of our Lord Jesus Christ, even the best the human race has achieved is not good enough, but certainly only the best is acceptable.

Now the question arises, how can we tell what is "best"? Are our standards merely subjective? Are they based on objective considerations? Are they merely the product of artistic snobbery and esoteric exclusiveness? These are legitimate questions, and deserve thoughtful answers. Before taking up the problem of what is worthy to be offered to God in the realm of the arts, especially in poetry and music, let us look at the cultural situation which confronts us all as Americans. We are in an era of mass culture, where mass standards are deplorably low in many fields. In spite of some encouraging signs, America still seems like a nation of lowbrows. Anyone who tries to represent the truly first-rate finds that he is working against inertia if not outright opposition. Americans lead the world in many things, but not yet in an intelligent appreciation and support of artistic excellence. Why is this? Oswald Spengler has one rather provocative explanation.

In his *Decline of the West,* Spengler maintains that the keenest and most vigorous individuals in any civilization are attracted into those activities which currently seem to be making most progress, and in which there is the most creative excitement. For instance, at the beginning of the sixteenth century, the Church of Rome had, as one historian puts it, the pick of the "most fabulous array of talent ever available in any one place at any one time" for the enrichment of her cultural life. This was the Italy of Pope Julius II; at his accession in 1503, Leonardo da Vinci was still at work in Florence, as were Michelangelo, Perugino and his young pupil Raphael. Botticelli was fifty-nine, Perugino fifty-seven, Leonardo fifty-one, Michelangelo twenty-eight and Raphael twenty. Others working in the city were Lorenzo di Credi, Fra Bartolommeo, Filippino Lippi and the man whom Vasari called "the perfect painter," Andrea del Sarto. Francia was in Bologna, Pinturicchio in Siena, Luini in Milan. Venice could boast Mantegna, Bellini, Carpaccio, Giorgione, Palma Vecchio, and Titian.[2] A young man with any artistic skill at all was likely to be caught up in the whirlwind of creative energy which produced the sculpture, painting, architecture, and decoration which have been the wonders of the world ever since.

Somewhat the same thing occurred from time to time in Germany, in the realm of *music:* in the eighteenth century at the time of Bach, and especially in the nineteenth, during the heyday of the Romantic Movement, which produced, along with scores of lesser lights, Beethoven, von Weber, Schubert, Schumann, Mendelssohn, Brahms, Liszt, Wagner and Richard Strauss. It has often been said that anyone who went out to an evening party in those days, who was handed a piece of music to read and sing at sight and who begged off by saying that he did not know how to read music, would have been looked on as almost as much of a curiosity as a guest today who said he could not read. The educated public appreciated and supported music.

This public understanding and enjoyment was the soil which nourished the seeds of genius, and brought them to fruition. In neither sixteenth-century Italy nor nineteenth-century Germany was it primarily the hope of riches which attracted the young and able into artistic pursuits, though in many cases patronage promised a living; some artists, composers and performers died poor. The hope of fame lured a few; but probably for most it was the excitement and satisfaction of being identified with enterprises which offered conspicuous self-fulfillment and which seemed to the majority gloriously worthwhile.

Nineteenth-century America was chiefly absorbed in the subjugation and exploitation of the continent; therefore most vigorous citizens of the time were attracted in some way to activities bearing upon the conquest of nature and the development of the machine. The United States, so Spengler's argument might run, has never been a place where large numbers of enterprising men have been powerfully lured by the arts. Art has been considered by many a secondary concern of society: a trimming, a decoration, an embroidery on life, rather than as something basic or central. Devotion to the arts in America has been somewhat self-conscious, the devotees apologetic, insecure, and often belligerently sensitive to criticism. Only recently has the picture been changing, with more people becoming intelligently interested in architecture, literature and music. Abstract painting still has hard sledding with the average American, as does contemporary poetry, atonal music and symbolic drama. But the classics are having an encouraging revival; and, along with many evidences of aesthetic insensitivity, bad taste, the cultivation of the tough and uncouth in manners, dress and speech, we must admit that more Americans than ever before in history know something about great painting and great music.

Until quite recently, artistic taste correlated somewhat with socio-economic status, so that the wealthy on the eastern seaboard, who could travel to Europe from time to time, were more apt to go in for what was thought to be "cultural" than the business, industrial or farming communities of the Middle West. In a pluralistic society such as ours, it is quite impossible to do justice to the complexities of the subject without treating it at great length and in considerable depth, but the bearing of these matters on the life of our churches can easily be seen.

Forty years ago I lived in a small residential community, where half the men worked in a nearby city and the other half were employed in the town to supply the needs of the commuters. The Episcopal and the Presbyterian Churches were supported chiefly by the college-graduate, commuting, country-club set. The Methodist, Baptist and United Presbyterian Churches ministered largely to those who lived and worked in the town. The African Methodist Episcopal Church was the social and religious center of the community's Negro population. The Roman Catholic Church embraced a far wider social spectrum than any of the others, but still did not include many well-to-do families. The striking thing was the difference in the nature of the preaching, the type of public worship, and the standard of the music in the various Protestant congregations. The society weddings were almost inevitably held in the Episcopal or the Presbyterian churches. There the preaching was literate and liberal; the services were dignified and rich in poetry; the music was tasteful. The Methodist, Baptist, and United Presbyterian congregations were made up of hard working people with few cultural pretensions. The furnishings of those sanctuaries were of golden oak. The services were more informal, the prayers extemporaneous, the congregational singing enthusiastic. In the African Methodist Episcopal Church the preaching and praying were fervent, the singing heart-felt and full-throated. And, whereas in the well-to-do churches one heard anthems of a fairly high quality, well sung by paid quartets, in the others, volunteer singers frequently rendered "selections" which featured sentimental words set to technically inferior music. The hymnals ranged all the way from good to mediocre to poor. There were some hymns which were used by all the Protestant churches: "Old hundredth," "Come, thou almighty King," "Holy, holy, holy," "When I survey the wondrous cross," "Dear Lord and father of mankind," "Jerusalem the golden." One would never sing "Shall we gather at the river?" or "Throw out the lifeline" in the Episcopal or Presbyterian services, or "All creatures of our God and King" or "We gather together to ask the Lord's blessing" in the Negro church. If one wished to hear really spirited singing, however, the evening services at the Methodist or the African Methodist churches were the ones to attend. Here one could enjoy "In the sweet by and by," "What a friend we have in Jesus," "Bringing in the sheaves," "Sweet hour of prayer," "Safe in the arms of Jesus"; and in the Negro congregation chiefly, "Swing low, sweet chariot," "I got shoes," "Go down, Moses," as well as "Brighten the corner where you are," "Blessed assurance," and other spirituals and revival hymns.

It would have been quite impossible to explain to those whose hymns consisted chiefly of "inferior" words set to "sentimental" music, featuring the liberal use of sub-dominant chords, diminished sevenths and secular rhythms, that there was anything inappropriate about worshipping God in this manner. The whole concept of worship as an offering or oblation to God would have been difficult to make clear. God was conceived as a Familiar Friend who entered into the everyday lives of his people, who was the unseen Guest at every table, the Companion of their days and nights, a God of justice who frowned upon sin but also a Loving Father who understood and forgave, and who needed no intermediary between himself and the individual soul. You felt better for going to church and singing "Tell me the old, old story." You felt closer to God when the minister prayed from his heart in his own words rather than out of a book or in the language of lyric poetry. The kind of service that did you good was homey, folksy, intimate, plain, direct and familiar. The decorous, dimly lit, stained-glass atmosphere of the well-to-do sanctuaries where you never sang too loud or prayed too long, where hired professional musicians rendered "long-haired" music while ushers took up the collection, where the sermons were filled with polysyllables and references to the latest popular novels as well as the literary classics of the English-speaking world, where no one put on any "rousements," and everyone was continually on his best behavior, did not appeal to the common man in that town. How could you express joy in your gratitude at having been "saved by the blood of the Lamb" in such subdued and artificial surroundings? How could a preacher let himself go, when the Spirit moved him, against the sins of a wicked world under those conditions?

And, when we come to think of it, how can anyone be sure that God is not far more in favor of the uninhibited, friendly approach of "popular" religion than he is by the more formal and externally more reverent demeanor of the well-educated worshipper?

Of course, with the Roman Catholics, the situation was quite different. There was no *congregational* singing in the sanctuary itself, although plenty of singing at Communion breakfasts in the parish house. The solemn service of the Mass emphasized the concept of a God High and Lifted Up, to be approached through his Church and his priests in utter reverence, the sacrifice of whose Son actually took place again upon the altar whenever the Mass was said. The Latin of the liturgy bound the people of the twentieth century to those of the past. The great, unbroken stream of thought and life embraced each generation in turn. The plain-song of the Gregorian chant by soloist or choir served to reinforce the atmosphere which altar, ritual, candles, incense, and dimness established. Worship here *was* a sacrifice, and oblation. The folksiness of much Catholic popular devotion was reserved for meetings *outside* the sanctuary, where good fellowship often expressed itself in ways just as secular and sentimental as anything Protestantism at its worst could boast, but in the church itself, no! Of course, it must be admitted that if artistic standards are to be measured by the statuary, the stained glass windows, even the altar itself, these standards were low. The general effect of nave, choir, chancel was medieval, mysterious, but many of the individual details, such as the colored images, were, when studied closely, as "corny" as the golden oak of Protestant furnishings. Now, forty years later, this is being changed. Catholic architects and craftsmen are in the forefront of the movement for better ecclesiastical art, often ahead of their Protestant counterparts; but in those days, this was not the case.

There are encouraging signs that American churches are waking up to their opportunity in the artistic field, but they still have a long way to go. One has only to make a study of the four-page leaflets in which the order of morning worship and the announcements for the week are printed or mimeographed. These leaflets often have an illustration or design on the cover. They are put out by publishing houses by the thousands; when the individual pastor receives them, they are blank, except for the cover-picture. From the artistic point of view it is rather depressing to survey what is actually being distributed. The churches lag behind many other institutions which use commercial art. Sunday Schools go in for religious "comics." Pastors send out annual Christmas letters adorned by poorly drawn, highly colored, tasteless illustrations. Framed reproductions purchased with good money for the parish house are often of inferior quality. And it is a rather sad commentary on the state of Protestant artistic taste that the "most widely favored portrait of Christ ever painted," the reproduction of which keeps "multi-color presses" operating around the clock "to meet the demand," is that of Warner Sallman. Even though this is not as bad as other similar studies by Jambor, Pusecker, and Howard Chandler Christy, the elongated, blue-eyed effeminacy of the face makes many sensitive people wince; and yet sixty million reproductions of the painting have been made and circulated.

In thinking about these matters, it is, of course, important to keep one's perspective. The Christian Gospel is a gospel of salvation, and a Christian's level of esthetic appreciation has very little, if anything, to do with his appreciation of salvation. It is impossible to prove that a taste for good music, painting, sculpture, poetry, drama, architecture and decoration brings a person any nearer to the attitude appropriate to the humble servant of the Living God, the fostering of which is the Church's chief concern. It may even be that extreme artistic fastidiousness, with its concomitant absorption in problems of esthetic standards, has a tendency to breed a form of cultural snobbery which militates against a genuine sympathy for all of God's children. After all, a person who thinks Sallman's "Head of Christ" is "inspiring," who loves the poetry of Edgar Guest and the sound of "the Rosary" played on an electronic organ, may still have a far surer grasp of the fundamentals of the Gospel than one who turns up his nose at these things.

As David Manning White points out in *Mass Culture* there is no necessary correlation between national culture and civic virtue or democratic feeling. In Germany, music was patronized as never before in history: German youth were taught to recite and quote from the works of Goethe, Schiller and Lessing, and yet, "with all this cultural buttress its best seller of all time was *Mein Kampf*, with its ten million copies." [3] Germany fell for Hitler in spite of her high level of culture; and it does not follow that America is necessarily doomed, morally and spiritually, unless she is able to resist the inroads now being made by inferior mass culture. "There was nothing to preclude an Ilse Koch," Mr. White observes, "from listening to the Second Brandenburg Concerto on her gramophone while she practiced her hobby of tanning the human skin of some unfortunate Jew who was placed in Belsen. We are told she made lamp shades of some of the skins. . . . Misanthropy and race hatred can be the common heritage of a musical genius like Wagner or a political demagogue like Senator Bilbo. No one could applaud the exquisite work of the Ballet at the Bolshoi Theater louder and longer than Comrade Stalin, but his appreciation of the arts did not stand in the way of the most utter ruthlessness. To equate sane and beneficent government with *haute culture* is to open a magic casement upon a scene that has no real basis in man's experience."

On the other hand, this line of argument should never be made the excuse for neglecting to offer God, in his church, the best that our civilization affords. If education is the introduction of the immature to the spiritual possessions of the race, it is a dereliction of duty for a teacher to expose students to anything less than the best. If religion is concerned with the whole of life and is out to save the whole man, we should not think of God as concerned merely with the "soul" and not with the mind, the emotions, the tastes, and the standards of humanity. It has been frequently pointed out that Christianity is deeply interested in *both* body and spirit; it takes seriously our physical life in a real world of "material" objects, even though we now know that "material" does not mean "solid" in the old Democritean sense.

The stimulating brochure entitled *The Church, the Arts, and Contemporary Culture* [4] begins: "The full scope of Christian life and work inevitably includes attention to the arts in all their contemporary forms. . . . The arts, old and new, good and bad, are peculiarly the carriers of meaning and value in our society as in all societies. Thus the arts and the meanings symbolized and communicated have obvious religious and theological significance." The five main points made in the statement are as follows:

"1. The first task of the Church in the area of the arts is to know contemporary culture and its expressions and through them to know our time more fully."

"2. The second task of the Church in the area of the arts is to assess and interpret them in terms of Christian criteria."

"3. A third task of the Church in the area of the arts is

to contribute directly to the health and vitality of the arts and the proper understanding of the vocation of the artist."

"4. A fourth task of the Church in the area of the arts is to heal the breach that has arisen between the religous institution and those chiefly identified with the arts in our society."

"5. A final task of the Church in the area of the arts is to bear witness to the common ground to which both religion and the arts refer."

It is obvious that those who framed this statement for the National Council of Churches believe strongly that God is concerned that his people shall come to grips with what the arts have said and are saying, and shall use only the most meaningful in his service. This, if taken seriously, means that everything done by Christians for the building of the Church visible and the carrying on of its tradition of worship and fellowship shall be as expressive as it can possibly be made, and especially that it shall avoid the trashy, the sham, the pseudo, the sentimental, and the pretentious. The Church must not lag behind other institutions in understanding and appropriating what the great cultural movements of the past and present have to offer. The fostering of good art is the way to drive out the bad. When the Church insists that every artistic decision she makes is a welcome opportunity to give up the ineffective for the effective, the mediocre for the excellent, the sentimental for the powerful, the apparent for the real, the stale for the vital and the weak for the strong, the tone of her life and witness will improve. The Living God of truth, goodness and beauty will be more fittingly worshipped. This does not mean that the average churchgoer may not still be powerfully and adversely affected by the crudities of our mass culture or that he may be restive if the Church stands for something which seems to him unfamiliar and esoteric. But the hope lies in the steady exposure of the younger members to types of architecture, painting, poetry, literature, hymns, anthems, organ music, and drama which measure up to the finest standards, embraced by the most creative and thoughtful Christians, so that gradually they come to develop a taste for excellence which will lead them in turn to discard the mediocre. God in his omniscience understands the conditioning which each person has suffered or enjoyed, and therefore does not "blame" anyone for preferring Edgar Guest to John Keats, or Ethelbert Nevin to Healy Willan. One does not create a desire for better poetry or music by making fun of those who prefer doggerel or "tunes." One creates a desire by introducing people to something excellent, but something which still makes connections with their past experience, and gradually helps them to develop enough understanding to appreciate what the superior work of form or color or sound is trying to say. Anyone who can hum "The Palms" can follow Bach's "Jesu thou joy of man's desiring." Anyone who likes "I need thee every hour" can easily come to appreciate "My faith it is an oaken staff," which is a far stronger composition. It is the *leadership* of the Church which must insist upon high standards if the *laity* is to be helped. If "the hungry sheep look up and are not fed," it is the minister's responsibility. But far more than a duty is the privilege of helping people worship not only in the "beauty of holiness" but in the holiness of beauty.

A most interesting illustration of a cultural leader who insists that high standards are theologically mandatory is Archibald Thompson Davison, formerly professor of music at Harvard. Dr. Davison has written two extraordinarily influential books: *Protestant Church Music in America,* and

Church Music, Illusion and Reality. In his second book the author reappraises the situation in the Protestant Churches (other than the Protestant Episcopal Church) with which he had dealt in detail in the first book. In the preface to the second, he states his disappointment that more progress has not been made in the improvement of church music between the appearance of the two volumes. He acknowledges that some churches do "live by a high musical standard" but that these represent a "lamentably small minority"; and that his criticism of the inferior quality of music in the average church does not spring from "prejudice or caprice" but is based on "technical considerations" and upon "esthetic and religious conviction." He admits that "it may seem to the reader that in its zeal for dignity and artistic worth this book is intractably professional and fantastically purist. To such an objection the author can only say that in his opinion no man to whom the God he worships is perfect with a perfection that transcends human imagining could be held sincere did he not, to the utmost, maintain toward church music the most inflexibly purist ideals reinforced by every critical faculty he possesses."[5]

Dr. Davison insists that music is music, and that intrinsically there is no difference between religious and secular music. "Music, taken by itself, and at its fullest capacity, can never be an apologist for anything save beauty." But music acquires associations, and when music which is normally associated with secular activities—dancing, marching, serenading, love-making, toasting, and so forth—or when it immediately suggests comedy or sport or battle or labor, it is inappropriate for use in the church. Worship in the sanctuary should be solely for "the glory of God, not for any of the psychological, social, opportunistic, or utilitarian ends for which our worship music is now tortured out of its true nature, but as an offering, a sacrifice, a return in kind of God's gift of beauty to man."[6] "I see no prospect of extensive improvement in church music . . . until by purging it of its worldly substance we make of it something that is uniquely the music of worship."[7]

How, according to Dr. Davison, can this purging be done? What are the hurdles we should make music jump before it is fit for the sanctuary? What are the criteria by which we can distinguish between appropriate and inappropriate music for worship? There are six tests which can be applied; they involve matters of rhythm, melody, counterpoint, chromaticism, dissonance and modality. The author's analysis of these features of music is technical, and is treated at greater length in his first book than in his second. But even for a mere layman in the musical realm, the criteria are not too difficult to understand.

He simply means that music for worship should not have the kind of *rhythm* (be it three-four, six-eight, two-four or four-four) which suggests waltzing, marching, the fox-trot, the one-step, the polka, or jitterbugging! This automatically eliminates "Onward, Christian soldiers," "Shall we gather at the river?," "Pass me not, O gentle savior," "Throw out the life-line," "When the roll is called up yonder, I'll be there," "When the saints go marching in," and so forth.

Nor should church music (either in hymns, anthems, offertories, preludes or postludes) have the kind of melodies which we think of as immediately singable *tunes,* whether lively or sad, striking or sentimental, and which immediately suggest some secular activity. This would conceivably eliminate "What a friend we have in Jesus," "Sun of my soul," "Tell me the old, old story," and, for anthems, "The Lost Chord," "The Palms," and Parker's "Jerusalem."

Actually, *counterpoint* rather than harmony suggests the

austerity and dignity desirable in church music. Thus plainsong or simple countrapuntal compositions would seem more suitable than beautiful melodies, with a rich harmonic accompaniment.

Chromaticism, according to Dr. Davison, should be avoided, because of its sentimental connections with secular love-songs and mood-music. It is the chromaticism of the tune *Rest,* to which "Dear Lord and Father of mankind" is normally sung, which gives it a flavor inappropriate for objective worship. The half-tone intervals of both the first and second bars represent an insinuating sweetness out of place in the church, even though permissable on a picnic or at an informal "sing." It is the chromaticism of the inner voices, together with the repetitive sequences of the melody and the slow waltz-rhythm, which renders *Galilee* ("Jesus calls us; o'er the tumult") unacceptable, according to Dr. Davison.

On the other hand, the arresting *dissonances* of many contemporary anthems suggest, according to our author, extra-ecclesiastical moods and hence render them unfit for the church.

Finally, the ideal might be *modal* music, in the Gregorian idiom, rather than that employing the more familiar diatonic scale. This severs all connections with secular activities in the modern world, and renders modal music particularly suitable for the reinforcement and heightening of the words of liturgy, litany or psalm.

A clear statement of the view of God which Dr. Davison does not accept, and which he feels much of what goes on in Protestant worship-services implies, is found in his earlier book: "We behave in His (God's) house as though He were a friendly sort of host who, although He is God, would prefer to be treated like one of us. So we build our churches like halls; our pulpits like office desks; we must hear modernized versions of the Scriptures which sound vulgar, but which are only stupid; we won't kneel when the minister prays because God, being a democratic God, respects our independence and doesn't ask such servility; we won't intone a service because a man doesn't sing to his father, he talks to him. Whatever may be the merit of such an attitude, it may be stated in behalf of a high standard of church music that no great art has ever issued from any concept of God as the Supreme Benign Rotarian."[8]

Dr. Davison, in an interesting passage at the beginning of this same book, begs us to believe that he is not indulging in mere highbrowism or snobbery when he takes such a puristic attitude towards ninety percent of what the Protestant Churches normally use as music. He claims that his own musical inclinations outside the church are thoroughly "catholic." "I proclaim," he writes, "my delight in jazz, Wagner, Gilbert and Sullivan, Hindemith, Jerome Kern, Schumann, and Johann Strauss, but I cannot conscientiously entertain any of these gentlemen within the doors of the church."[9] We are not told, in either of Dr. Davison's books, what he thinks about *religious* songs for use at conferences, retreats, hymn-sings, young peoples' meetings, informal singing around the piano, summer camp vesper services, and so forth. His criteria are primarily designed to help determine the music which is appropriate to the formal worship of God "in his holy temple." I believe we can sympathize with his feeling that all parts of the service, if worship be considered an oblation, should be composed of elements which humble men may appropriately use to acknowledge the sovereignty of an Infinite Deity of Goodness, Truth, and Beauty. We may, and I for one do, differ with Dr. Davison at certain points on what constitutes appropriateness in sacred music; for instance, I do not believe that we need be as completely restricted, as he feels one should be, to the use of triadic harmony, and the elimination of dissonance from music used in worship. I know that my own children, brought up on the sacred music of Poulenc, Benjamin Britten, Honegger and Bloch, are not at all distracted by the "strangeness" of the harmony used by these composers, nor would they feel that it fostered exclusively secular connotations. But I do agree that in church it is right to offer only what we believe to be first-rate, and in keeping with the solemnity of the occasion and the nature of the Deity. We will not go far wrong if we concentrate on these things.

I am chiefly concerned about our concept of God, the concept which we have in our minds as we approach him; but I wonder whether those who make such a point of the solemnity and dignity of worship fully realize what they are implying. Are they not assuming that God is a Power whose dignity is offended if he is not given sufficient honor? It may be that God wants us to honor him in humility and contrition because that is the only way in which we as sinful creatures should behave in his presence; but as to his own being, one is permitted to doubt whether he worries about how he is praised, worshipped or addressed. After all, a truly great *human being* is not worried about being given his due to the extent that some people worry about *God's* being given his; and if God is so much better than we, "as the heavens are higher than the earth," is it not possible to imagine him as completely removed from all concern about what people think of him, *except* as he realizes that a reverential attitude on the part of man is a true indication of proper humility? The Power behind the

Universe surely does not have to be on his dignity like an oriental potentate; and some of those who treat him as a Cosmic Pal may be paying him a compliment which he appreciates. We do not really know enough to judge others in this matter any more than we know enough to judge others morally. For my own part, it would be completely out of keeping with all that I know of our faith to think of God first of all as anything but awe-inspiring, infinite, omniscient, omnipotent; but I also recognize the validity of the other locus of the ellipse: the Father's infinite understanding and forgiving love for his children. The Christian view of God is paradoxical to the extent that no *one* concept does full justice to the way he deals with us or appeals to us at *all* times and at *all* stages of our experience.

There are, however, several issues still to be faced in the realm of religion and music. It is possible to become disturbed by the quality of hymns and anthems used in church; but when musicians criticize "Dear Lord and Father of mankind" for its somewhat sentimental chromaticism, and "Blest be the tie that binds" because of its waltz-sequences, they should realize how *relatively* minor a problem this is compared to the mediocrity of the repertoire which is actually being used both in and out of the churches. America is being saturated with "popular" religious songs so far inferior to the two hymns mentioned above as to make these and others like them seem "classical." They are sung on "revival" hour radio programs as well as in churches; they are being introduced into countless young peoples' society meetings, Sunday evening "gospel" services, summer conferences. They appear on national television programs. Records of them, both as individual discs and long-playing albums, are selling in the millions. What about the "religious education" the American public is getting from all this? What concepts of God are being popularized throughout the land?

Leaving aside the fine old genuine spirituals, we should distinguish carefully between the various types of popular religious songs. *First,* there are the pseudo-hymns set to marching or dancing rhythms, and sometimes played by dance-orchestras or by bands in parades, like "When the saints go marching in," or "The old time religion." The former is only twenty years old, the latter is a "spiritual"; and many of the rhythmic imitations of spirituals fall into this category. *Second,* there are the evangelistic songs used in large revival meetings, particularly on the West Coast, but also in other parts of the country, such as "Sound the battle cry," "Brighten the corner where you are," "Blessed assurance," "The old rugged cross." *Third,* there are the jazzy revival songs like "Assurance march" (the music, without any change, would make a stirring football song), and "The royal telephone" ("We may talk to Jesus thru the royal telephone"). *Fourth,* there are the "commercial" religious songs like "He," where the music is usually a sentimental waltz or a very slow fox-trot. *Fifth,* there are the lively "commercial" religious songs like "Have you talked to the Man Upstairs?" and "Way out beyond the blue." *Sixth,* there are the musical comedy songs sometimes used in a religious way, like "You'll never walk alone" from *Carousel* by Rodgers and Hammerstein. *Seventh,* there is a miscellaneous class of pseudo-Christmas, Easter, Sabbath songs vaguely celebrating seasons or the tenuous spirituality of general good will, the desirability of going to church, or the idea that if we only have faith everything will come out right in the end.

The theology expressed in the words of these compositions is as various as the types themselves. The *first three* groups are based upon fundamentalist concepts: inerrant scripture, propitiatory atonement, with a strong emphasis on the after-life, heaven, hell, judgment, immortality. In the revival-hour song-books I have studied, almost one third of the selections are concerned with salvation after death: "This world is not my home," "Hallelujah, we shall rise," "We'll soon be done with trouble and trials," "At the end of the road," "The eastern gate," "In the sweet by and by," "Only glory by and by," "We're marching to Zion," "When mine eyes behold the King," and scores of others. Other themes are the heinousness of sin and the saving power of Jesus, especially through his atoning blood, whereby forgiveness is secured and heaven is won.

The *fourth* and *fifth* types of songs are based upon an entirely different concept of God and religion. In these, for the most part, God is considered an approachable Friend, not one in any sense to be feared, who is with us wherever we go, and who makes no very serious demands on his children. Here we find no great emphasis upon sin, only upon human weakness and fallibility, easily forgiveable. Immortality is assumed, but salvation comes from God's generous tolerance not from the acceptance of a sacrifice made for us by Christ. These songs are theistic, optimistic, sentimental. The last two types have no common denominator and no common theology; most of them assume a vague Spirit that makes for goodness, and, though the road may be steep and the night long, the dawn is bound to come soon.

None of these types fit any definition of a good hymn (effective lyric poetry set to worthy music) or meet the theological requirements of liberal evangelical Christianity; and it is extraordinarily difficult to take people who have been brought up on this kind of music and lead them to a real appreciation of something finer. Yet it is the duty of everyone, according to his lights and convictions, to be an educator and even an evangelist for higher standards; while engaged in this task, let him not forget to scrutinize the ideas of the Deity which are being set forth, often unconsciously, and to insist that people *think* about what they sing and hear and use as vehicles for their prayer and praise. An intelligent Christian should show that he loves God not only with his heart and soul and strength, but also with his *mind.*

CHAPTER 10

Man's Image and God's

In the first chapter of Genesis, it is written that God said, "Let us make man in our image (Hebrew: *tselem*), after our likeness (Hebrew: *demuth*)." If this is what God actually did, something of his nature can be known from a study of man. Some might qualify this by saying that it is from a study of man at his *best* that we get a clue to the nature of God; Christians maintain that it is from a study of *Jesus*—surely man at his best—that we get the clearest conception of the divine nature. But the Old Testament indicates that man—any man, or man in general—can furnish a clue in so far as his essential being is concerned, for that being is characterized by personality and self-awareness. It is therefore the nature of man's self-conscious spirit rather than the moral character of any particular man that can be thought of as a *tselem* or *demuth* of the Divine. Man as a free being, apart from how he uses his freedom, furnishes a hint concerning at least one indispensable element in our thought of God.

However, when we confront the way historic man has, for the most part, used his freedom, we have a much harder time visualizing him as in any sense akin to the Divine: he seems more demonic than godlike. Many of the most powerful modern dramas present the seamy side of human nature in clinical detail, leaving us shocked and sobered. We are not helped to think of God as Father by the four hours' exposure we get to James Tyrone, the head of the family in O'Neill's *Long Day's Journey into Night;* and, after having known the Big Daddy of Tennessee Williams' *Cat on a Hot Tin Roof,* we could easily sympathize with his son, Brick, for not being attracted to the idea of divine fatherhood at all.

A well-known *bon vivant* recently wrote to a New York newspaper criticizing the statement of a correspondent that "man is the highest form of life on this world." He writes, "Can he with a straight face look at the front page of any daily newspaper and then blandly make that assertion? For sheer superiority in the every form of morality, good breeding, gentle instincts and every imaginable aspect of goodness and manners, my dog Towser has it over the human race like a tent. . . . 'Man is the highest form' is the comedy line of all time."

On November 14, 1955, John Graham Gilbert confessed to taking out $37,500 worth of insurance on his mother's life, and then placing a bomb in the airplane in which she was to ride. The plane later exploded and killed forty-four people.

In October, 1957, three teen-age boys admitted torturing and killing two cats and four kittens and were sent to the National Training School in Washington for indefinite periods. The mother of the fourteen-year-old ringleader was dying of cancer in a hospital. The judge who handed down the sentences told the boy's father, "I hope your wife doesn't have to know about this," to which the father replied, "I'm glad she doesn't."

The horrible things people do, and the things we do or are tempted to do, make it very difficult to believe that man is, as Jean-Jacques Rousseau and Confucius both believed, *essentially* good. If man is not essentially good, how can he be, in any reasonable sense, a clue to the nature of God?

A high official in the Nazi regime fell in love with a married woman; on a trumped-up charge he had her husband put in prison, but in such a way that the husband was not conscious of the official's being behind the action; the Nazi then persuaded the husband to make over his property to his wife; he then released the husband from prison after persuading the wife to divorce the husband and marry him; then he got his new wife to make over her property to him; then he divorced her. In what sense could he be an image of anyone but the devil?

Orthodox Christianity speaks about the "Fall" and "original sin" as an explanation of the tendency in man to affirm his own life at the expense of other life and his independence as over against dependence on God; but surely this is highly symbolic and poetical. This is not an "explanation." Possibly biology is nearer to the truth when it maintains that many of the capacities which once were necessary for the continuance of the race are the very ones which, in a closely knit and competitive society, get man into trouble, and cause the strife, confusion, suffering, unhappiness and dislocation which we call evil, and which we attribute to the workings of man's "sinful" nature. The neo-orthodox theologians have, for the most part, completely neglected this approach to human perversity, intractability and intransigeance. This does not answer the philosophical question of *why* the natural man in the natural order *had* to develop in this way, but it does point to factors which, if left out of account, leave us with very little but mythical elements to "explain" the human predicament. The anthropoids who were equipped with the proper hair-trigger nervous response to fight or flee when confronted with danger survived and propagated; those animals not properly equipped suffered extinction and left no progeny. But the same aggressive traits which guaranteed survival must be highly modified, redirected or sublimated if they are to help an individual in the twentieth century. Looking into our own hearts we at once can see what we have inherited: we want what we want when we want it, and we don't want anyone to tell us what to do, unless we come to the point of craving security so much that we are willing to exchange our desire for independence for the safe feeling of being taken care of; and, even so, it is all in the interests of our precious *selves*. However, we are never completely content to resign ourselves to egoism and egotism. The drive towards mutual aid in the animal world is as "natural" as the impulses of self-protection and propagation. As humans, we hear, within our hearts, the still small voice, the urge to be more unselfish, more humble, more obedient, more loving; and it is this side of human nature which gives a hint of what the divine nature must be. The religious man believes that these promptings toward the higher life come from the Ultimate Power behind the universe, and hence are indicative of the essential character of that Power. We could derive the notion of a Deity who is personal and self-aware from the belief that man was made in the image of God, but we derive the notion of a good Deity from a recognition of the promptings towards the ideal within the human heart. So the image of ourselves as we believe we ought to be is accepted by the devout as inspired by One who is forever the perfection towards which we strive but never attain.

Walter M. Horton recommends that we "adopt the hypothesis which is the most natural of all hypotheses: that man is growing up under the tutelage of a Person or Persons greatly superior to him in wisdom and goodness."[1] But, he says, "We do not take God all at once; the mind could not grasp so great a concept . . . we project before us that image of God which most exactly corresponds with our own needs."[2] This is where the psychologist brings the imagination of man into the process. When a missionary told an old Chinese mother about the Christian conception of God, she exclaimed: "I've always thought there should be a God like that." A character in George Macdonald's *Robert Falconer* says: "If I only knew that God was as good as that woman, I should be content."

Toynbee maintains that, underneath the diversities of belief and practice found in the high religious of mankind, there is a common "attitude or spirit" which can be expressed in the words: "Man is not the spiritually highest presence known to man," and man should therefore try to achieve harmony with this higher presence by supporting the good against the evil in the world. Even in more general terms Whitehead predicts, "That religion will conquer which can render clear to popular understanding some eternal greatness incarnate in the passage of temporal fact." Montague says that true religion is based upon the conviction that what is highest in our experience is also deepest in the nature of things. And the agnostic André Malraux says, "The great mystery is not that we should have been thrown down here at random between the profusion of matter and that of the stars; it is that, from our very prison, we should draw from our own selves images powerful enough to deny our nothingness." Malraux may mean primarily the images created by the great artists which somehow challenge man's acceptance of himself as mean and impermanent; but the statement might also, in other contexts, mean both a bracing vision of man as he might be and of God as he must be to be truly God.

We have seen that Man's images of the Divine vary from the highly personal and anthropomorphic to the extremely general and abstract. Christopher Fry has one of his characters in *The First-born* call God the "infinite eavesdropper." Conrad Gesner, the first modern mountain-climber, in explaining the lure of the Alps, speaks of how one is lifted up by contemplating the works of the "supreme Architect." Francis Thompson writes of the "Hound of Heaven." Henry Theodore Rowe speaks of the new understanding man has of "Orderly Energy," which "some call Intelligence," and "some call God." Tolstoy's famous phrase is, "God is he without whom one cannot live," and Wordsworth speaks of a "presence . . . a sense sublime of something far more deeply interfused." And the contrast in images is not only between the more personal and the more impersonal; it is between the companionable, approachable, friendly and the absolute, infinite, awe-inspiring; and sometimes even between the kindly and the frightening.

In Kaufmann and Hart's *You Can't Take It With You,* Grandpa gathers his unusual family around him at the dining-table, looks up at the ceiling, and delivers himself of the following "grace":

"Well, sir, we've been getting along pretty good for quite a while now, and we're certainly much obliged. Remember, all we ask is to just go along and be happy in our own sort of way. Of course we want to keep our health but as far as anything else is concerned, we'll leave it to you. Thank you."

Then, just before the final curtain, he again gathers his brood together for dinner, and, looking up, prays:

"Well, sir, here we are again. We want to say thanks for everything you've done for us. Things seem to be going along fine. . . . . Of course the fireworks blew up, but that was Mr. De Pinna's fault—not yours. We've all got our health and as far as anything else is concerned we'll leave it to you. Thank you." The family in this remarkable play is held together by a deep affection, even though each member pursues his own hobbies in a weirdly eccentric manner. There is a wonderful give-and-take in the way the individuals adjust to each other. Love, kindness and tolerance create a warm atmosphere which spills out across the footlights and bathes the audience in its friendliness. God is an unseen, kindly Presiding Genius who keeps his children on a very loose tether and does not interfere in their lives too much. The image of the Deity here is not distinctively a Christian one; it is the image born of a tolerant theism which is saved from sentimentality by the saltiness of the characters and the sophisticated good humor of the play.

By way of sharp contrast, let us look at the God of the Reverend Mr. Brown in *Inherit the Wind,* the disturbing and fascinating drama about the Scopes trial, by Jerome Lawrence and Robert Lee. The minister's daughter is in love with the high school instructor who has been sent to jail, pending his trial for teaching evolution in defiance of the state law; the girl is therefore torn between her father's fundamentalist faith and her suitor's liberal views. The father thinks he sees a cloven hoof peeping out from under the teacher's trousers. If his daughter becomes infected, she will surely be damned. At the prayer-meeting in the town square, the night before the trial, the Rev. Mr. Brown works the crowd up to a religious frenzy by shouting: "Do we believe?"

All: "Yes!"

Brown: "Do we believe the Word?"

All: "Yes!"

Brown: "Do we believe the truth of the Word?"

All: "Yes!"

Brown: (*Pointing a finger toward the jail*) "Do we curse the man who denies the Word?"

All (*Crescendo, each answer mightier than the one before*): "Yes!"

Brown: "Do we cast out this sinner in our midst?"

All: "Yes!"

Brown: "Do we call down hellfire on the man who has sinned against the Word?"

All (*Roaring*): "Yes!"

Brown (*Deliberately shattering the rhythm, to go into a frenzied prayer, hands clasped together and lifted heavenward*): "O Lord of the Tempest and the Thunder! O Lord of Righteousness and Wrath! We pray that Thou wilt make a sign unto us! Strike down this sinner, as Thou didst Thine enemies of old, in the days of the Pharaohs! (Brady—the counterpart of William Jennings Bryan—*shifts uncomfortably in his chair; this is pretty strong stuff, even for him.*) Let him feel the terror of Thy sword! For all eternity, let his soul writhe in anguish and damnation—"

Rachel (Brown's daughter): "No!" (*She rushes to the platform.*) "No, Father. Don't pray to destroy Bert!"

Brown: "Lord, we call down the same curse on those who ask grace for this sinner—though they be blood of my blood, and flesh of my flesh!"

Brady: (*Rising, grasping* Brown's *arm*) "Reverend Brown, I know it is the great zeal of your faith which makes you utter this prayer! But it is possible to be overzealous, to destroy that which you hope to save so that nothing is left but emptiness. Remember the wisdom of Solomon in the Book of Proverbs—(*Softly*) 'He that troubleth his own house . . . shall inherit the wind.'"

Here in this second play we have set forth two fundamentalist images of God; the one a God of wrath and vindictiveness, the other a God who, though demanding faith and obedience, nevertheless cannot be conceived as one who would destroy a man for heresy or unbelief. In regard to Mr. Brown's Deity, we can see why one can never say that to be a servant of God is *inevitably* a good thing, until we know the kind of God who is to be served. The more conscientious Mr. Brown was, the worse it was for the cause of true religion.

Then we have the Deity who requires quiet resignation. In *Pawns* by Percival Wilde, old Grigor finally realizes that the authorities require him and his sons to report to the faraway city for mobilization in World War I on the Russian side, and that his friendly neighbors must report to another city to enlist on the Austrian side because of the way the boundary-line between the two countries runs. Instead of protesting, he prays: "May we all be happy. May the dead reach God's kingdom. May we all be preserved in good health. Amen." And, making the sign of the cross, he takes up his pack and leaves to enlist.

Still another image is suggested in the third act of *Hamlet* where the Prince of Denmark, now completely convinced that his uncle murdered his father to get the crown and the queen, finds the villain at prayer. Claudius has been dreadfully disturbed in his conscience by seeing the play,

"The Murder of Gonzago," which, as amended by Hamlet, almost perfectly duplicates the king's own crime; he has already soliloquized:

"O, my offense is rank, it smells to heaven;
It hath the primal eldest curse upon 't,
A brother's murder. . . . What then? What rests?
Try what repentance can.—What can it not?
Yet what can it when one cannot repent? . . . .
Bow, stubborn knees, and, heart with strings of steel,
Be soft as sinews of the new-born babe!
All may be well." Claudius retires and kneels.

Hamlet enters and sees his uncle at prayer. He says: "Now might I do it pat, now he is praying," but he doesn't kill the king because he believes that he might send the villain's soul to heaven. He reasons that his uncle killed his father at a moment when the father was completely occupied with material things, "He took my father grossly, full of bread, with all his crimes, broad blown, as flesh as May," or, as the ghost admits himself, "with all my imperfections on my head." Hamlet would not get revenge by killing his uncle at prayer, so he decides to wait until his uncle reverts to type; Hamlet will kill him "When he is drunk asleep, or in his rage, or in the incestuous pleasure of his bed, at game, a-swearing, or about some act that has no relish of salvation in it; then trip him, that his heels may kick at heaven, and that his soul may be as damn'd and black as hell, whereto it goes." So Hamlet desists, and waits.

But the king, arising from his profitless praying, says:

"My words fly up, my thoughts remain below:
Words without thoughts never to heaven go."
The image of God implied here is interesting.

Claudius thinks for a moment that repentance may save him from damnation. Hamlet refuses to kill him because the King's repentance may entitle him to go straight to heaven. But the king realizes that he cannot repent unless he gets rid of what he gained by the murder of his brother: the crown, and the queen. He will not give these up, so he knows his prayer will do no good; God will hear his "words" but repudiate his "thoughts."

Although *Hamlet* is supposed to be about tenth-century Denmark, the ideology of the play is thoroughly Elizabethan. The theology of the time placed a great deal of emphasis on heaven and hell, and who went where and why. There are in Shakespeare's plays, over 700 references to "heaven" and over 150 to "hell." The importance of the moment when a person dies is emphasized several times. Hamlet's father was poisoned while taking an afternoon nap; he died before he could receive the last rites; he was "cut off even in the blossom" of his sin; and therefore his ghost is doomed to "walk the night," and by day to "fast in fires" until his murder is avenged. He tells his son that he is forbidden to reveal the secrets of his prison-house, but that if he could he would "unfold" a tale "which would harrow" Hamlet's soul, "freeze" his blood, make his eyes start from his head, and cause "each particular hair to stand on end." The chances are that he is speaking about a place with some of the characteristics of Purgatory because he believes he will be released from it and go to heaven when certain conditions are fulfilled. On the other hand, the Thirty-nine Articles of 1571 specifically label the idea of Purgatory as a "fond thing, vainly invented, and grounded upon no warranty of Scripture, but rather repugnant to the Word of God." So possibly we are supposed to imagine the ghost as coming from "hell." Purgatory is actually mentioned only twice in Shakespeare (once in *Romeo and Juliet* and once in *Othello*) and is not made much of in either instance. It is also well to remember that the whole episode of the ghost is more a literary device used for dramatic purposes than something which educated people would believe or which should be interpreted theologically. Nevertheless, it is still true that most Elizabethan Christians thought that a normally bad person might be a candidate for heaven if he died in a suddenly repentant mood, and Hamlet is said to believe this in the case of Claudius. The idea of God implied here is obvious and serves to set apart the faith of the early seventeenth century from that of the twentieth, although the importance still attached to extreme unction in the Roman Church testifies to the persistence of some of these conceptions.

Another feature of the seventeenth century which is still operative in modern Catholicism is the notion that the spiritual realm is peopled with many beings who can have some sort of contact with humans. The Mother Superior in Philip Barry's play *The Joyous Season* speaks far more often of Them than of Him. When she is disappointed at not receiving any light on the solution of a certain problem—light which she fully expected would come to her—during a Christmas service, she says, "I don't know what's the matter with Them up there."

This "Reverend Mother" is a member of a well-to-do Irish family who have come up in the world and are now living all together in a big house on Beacon Street. She has not seen any of them for years, but she arrives on Christmas eve for a visit. The oldest brother, who acts as the head of the family now that the parents are gone, is an upright, conservative citizen who accepts the "external leadership" of the Church. His faith is practical, and non-mystical. The wife of the second brother is a recent convert, and takes her religion more seriously than any of the others, with the exception of the Mother Superior herself. The neophyte follows Catholic customs meticulously, but does not seem to possess very much insight or to have achieved a real sense of freedom, although she is happier than she was before her conversion, because the great problems of life and destiny are now "settled." A younger brother is a social radical, inclined to be skeptical of mysticism of any sort; he interprets the "hunches" and "illuminations" which come to the charming "Reverend Mother" as due to telepathy.

But the "Reverend Mother" is one of those people who lives in continual and conscious contact with the unseen world. She looks up towards the ceiling when referring to spiritual beings. She believes she is guided by "Them." She prays to various saints, or rather "through" them, appealing to St. Jude, for instance, at a particularly critical juncture in the play. The saints and spirits are just as real to her as are the members of her own family. She is thoroughly convinced that "all things work together for good to them that love God," although her own mystical experience seems to be centered far more on God's helpers than on God himself.

This reminds one of the way in which Joan of Arc lived her life in constant dependence on the guidance and help of St. Catherine and St. Margaret. In Bernard Shaw's play, Joan is made to tell Captain Robert de Baudricourt, "It is the will of God that you are to do what He has put into my mind." Robert is puzzled by her statement that the saints speak to her every day.

Robert: "What did you mean when you said that St. Catherine and St. Margaret talked to you every day?"

Joan: "They do."

Robert: "What are they like?"

Joan (*suddenly obstinate*): "I will tell you nothing about that; they have not given me leave."

Robert: "But you actually see them; and they talk to you just as I am talking to you?"

Joan: "No, it is quite different. I cannot tell you; you must not talk to me about my voices."

Robert: "How do you mean? Voices?"

Joan: "I hear voices telling me what to do. They come from God."

Robert: "They come from your imagination."

Joan: "Of course. That is how the messages of God come to us."

Thus we see in the plays of Barry, the believer, and Shaw, the sympathetic skeptic, the same emphasis upon the perfect "naturalness" of God's dealing with the spiritually dedicated among his children: he often speaks through the saints, often directly, and no practical distinctions are indicated between the messages from God and those from lesser beings. It is through the imagination that the spiritual world impinges on our ordinary mental life, and not in some unnatural way.

As Malraux has said, we do "draw from our own selves images powerful enough to deny our nothingness" and this, he feels, is the "great mystery." But it is not so much a "mystery" to those who believe in God; if the Ground of All Being is in any sense conscious, self-aware, intelligent beyond our ability to conceive, and as concerned about us as Jesus said he is, then the very ability to conjure up images—whether in art, in personal life, or in religion—is God-given. And, for a Christian, the ultimate test of the validity of an image (of man as son or God as Father) is

Christ himself; this is a matter of faith, but it is not faith in spite of knowledge; it is faith that does not fear genuine knowledge whatever its source; it is faith that is enriched by knowledge.

John Baillie writes, "Jesus Christ is not another name for God, but the name of a Man in whom God was, and through whom God came to meet us. The Presence which indwells in the Christian's soul is always this God whom through Jesus we found."[3] But that is why we may feel that Grandpa's God in *You Can't Take It With You* lacks some of the challenge we find in the God of the New Testament, and why we may feel that the Rev. Mr. Brown's "Lord of the Tempest and the Thunder" in *Inherit the Wind* is not the same as the God revealed in Christ. The Christian God surely demands sincerity in prayer as Claudius acknowledged when he said that his words flew up while his thoughts remained below; and certainly the spiritual tone of the "Reverend Mother's" life in *The Joyous Season* is in harmony with the *quality* of the Christian image, even though we might not feel it necessary to imagine the unseen world as peopled with so many intermediaries, messengers and incorporeal agents as she did. Practically, it is the *attitude* produced by obedience to an image that is the crucial thing. The Christian image of God, at its best, should create in us an attitude of trustful *dependence* upon a Power holy and merciful, and of warm-hearted *goodwill* towards our fellow men, expressed in intelligent service. No one consistently achieves the humility and love recognized as ideal. We are all sinners; we all stand under God's judgment. But there are still tremendous differences between the cruel and the kind, the hardhearted and the sympathetic, the ego-centric and the helpful, the crooked and the honest; and so often the difference is reflected in the image of God which dominates the imagination, or the concept of the ultimate nature of the Universe which dominates the mind.

It is not only the images of art or the images of God but also our image of ourselves which can be "strong enough to deny our nothingness." There are many highminded agnostics today who are, from the Jewish-Christian standpoint, *better* than their "religion": that is, they conceive of man as having the potentiality to become an "image" of courage and understanding and sympathy *in spite of* what they consider the complete unconsciousness and indifference of the universe. They do not deny the demonic element in man; a few even affirm that the demonic, either gross or refined, is all there is to man: life is essentially a pitiful drama of sin and frustration lived out against the dark background of unthinking nothingness. But others believe that there can be an image of man which is noble, and they do their best to live up to it. Man may be defeated in the end but, for a moment, he glows with a pure incandescence of heart and mind; and this, for him and those who come within the orbit of his influence, makes life worth while. Obviously, in this case, even the heroic possibilities in man can give no clue to the ultimate nature of things. Man still is an accident, a sport, a mutation; but the image of himself as possessing the capacity to become honorable, decent and intelligent often is enough to make an agnostic want to become like the image.

But the true scientist is not apt to think of nature as a "dark background of unthinking nothingness." He may, or he may not, believe that the Ultimate Being has any concern for man but he usually feels a reverential awe towards the manifestations of that Being. The universe is magnificent. However it was created, its immensity, complexity, order and beauty are awe-inspiring; also eliciting our deep respect is the mind of an Einstein, who devised the formula that unlocked the energy of the atom: $e = mc^2$.

Published in *The New Yorker* was a bit of verse which contrasts this one certainty in nature with the uncertainties in other realms:

$$E = MC^2$$

BY MORRIS BISHOP

"What was our trust, we trust not;
What was our faith, we doubt;
Whether we must or must not,
We may debate about.
The soul, perhaps, is a gust of gas
And wrong is a form of right—
But we know that Energy equals Mass
By the Square of the Speed of Light."

"What we have known, we know not;
What we have proved, abjure;
Life is a tangled bowknot,
But one thing still is sure.
Come, little lad; come, little lass—
Your docile creed recite:
'We know that Energy equals Mass
By the Square of the Speed of Light.'" *

But, of course, there is more to the reliability of the universe than this one amazing formula. After all, it was the processes of the universe, however described or explained, which caused this planet to become habitable in the first place, and which nourished the development of all that we call civilization. Without the predictability of "material"

* Permission the author, © 1946 *The New Yorker Magazine*, Inc.

events, men would never have had a basis for their cultural life. The Jewish-Christian tradition has never, except when it has strayed down bypaths untrue to its real character, set spirit off against matter, and looked down upon "material" things as essentially unworthy. Man is psychosomatic; pigment reflects light at different wave-lengths to make art possible; sound travels in the atmosphere and, when the proper conditions of production and reception are fulfilled, becomes music. The deeper many scientists penetrate into the mysteries of the atom, the less "materialistic" become their hypotheses, the more dynamic seems the reality with which they try to deal. It is not, therefore, strange that so many physicists and astronomers are believers in a Super-Intelligent Power that was here before we came, will be here after we go, and which elicits a feeling of wonderment from those who spend much of their time studying the way nature behaves.

The trouble is, of course, that nature does not behave in ways that are always favorable to the pleasure, convenience or happiness of the individual human being. Nature punishes infraction of her "laws" even when committed in ignorance: a good man is poisoned when he mistakes a toadstool for a mushroom just as surely as a bad man. Nature does nothing to stop murders, massacres or the enslavement of the weak by the strong; hence, nature has a reputation for moral neutrality, except where certain physiological laws are involved: here she seems to favor prudence, moderation and common sense. Her capacities are ambiguous. The same power released by man can be a bane or a blessing. Atomic energy can propel ships and heat cities or sink ships and destroy cities. Nature, left to herself, seems to favor neither the one nor the other.

Now when God is conceived as the Ultimate Power who

expresses himself through nature and is in control of nature, one can see a genuine difficulty in this way of thinking. It looks as if God does not really care at all when people are buried under avalanches, struck by lightning, killed by tornadoes, drowned by floods, exterminated by epidemics; at least he does not seem to do anything to prevent these and similar catastrophes. If anything is to be done, man has to do it. It is man who has carved out a more abundant, comfortable and healthy life for himself by taking the ambiguous possibilities of the natural order and directing them into favorable channels. The natural order supplies the building blocks; man has to do the building. The natural order supplies the pieces of the picture-puzzle; man has to put them together. When man fights man, nature is neutral; so it must seem that the Power *behind* nature is neutral, or, if not neutral, then somehow powerless, or unwilling to intervene. Theists often argue that God *could* do anything, but does not interfere for certain good reasons of his own. This at times is terribly difficult for man to understand. One often sympathizes with Carlyle's bitter remark, "God sits in heaven and does nothing!"

For people of a simple religious faith, there are several ways out of this dilemma. One is to put down everything that happens which is favorable to man's health, happiness and development to the *direct action* of a Personal Deity, and everything unfavorable to the regularities of impersonal nature. Thus, one can be philosophical about a disease which strikes suddenly: this happens all the time, in the natural course of events, and does not need to be interpreted as evidence that God has singled the victim out for special punitive treatment. However, when one gets well, God is to be thanked. God is the author of every good and perfect gift; anything amiss is the luck of the draw.

Another way out of the difficulty is to imagine the world as a battleground between the forces of good and the forces of evil, between light and darkness, Ahura Mazda and Ahriman, God and Satan. The good can be attributed to God, the evil to the Devil. This is terribly hard to maintain, especially if it involves the frequently exploded notion that prosperity is the result of virtue and adversity the outcome of vice. The Bible, from Job on, keeps telling us that this is not so. A look around with open eyes gives no support to it either.

A few violent thinkers have gone to the other extreme and, concentrating on the injustices and unmerited tragedies of life, have excoriated God for creating a universe like ours. So James Thomson can rail,

> "That not for all Thy power furled and unfurled,
> For all the temples to Thy glory built,
> Would I assume the ignominous guilt
> Of having made such men in such a world!" [4]

In O'Neill's *All God's Chillun Got Wings,* Ella is contrite over what she has done to her husband, Jim. She asks him, whimpering, "Will God forgive me, Jim?" Jim answers, "Maybe He can forgive what you've done to me; and maybe He can forgive what I've done to you; but I don't see how He's going to forgive—Himself."

In a more ego-centric vein, Lord Londonderry could permit himself to write in his diary: "Here I learned that Almighty God, for reasons best known to himself, had been pleased to burn down my house in the county of Durham."

Beverly Nichols complains in *Sunlight on the Lawn:* "Why do insurance companies, when they want to describe an act of God, pick on something which sounds much more like an act of the Devil? One would think that God was exclusively concerned in making hurricanes, smallpox, thunderbolts and dry rot. They seem to forget that He also manufactures rainbows, appleblossoms and Siamese kittens."

Edward FitzGerald interprets Omar Khayyam as saying that he would like to "smash the scheme of things entire, and mould it nearer to the heart's desire." Dr. Fosdick suggests that if any attempt were made to do this, to construct a universe, different from the one we have and better planned, one would find it necessary to include: a dependable basis of regular law, the possibility of progress and development, a measure of real freedom for man, and community life as a matrix for his growth.[5] Then he proceeds to show how "these four things contain all the sources of our misery" as well as of our well-being.

Conceivably God could have created beings who did exactly as they were ordered. Puppets pulled by strings, however, could never satisfy his divine concern and love. But once God took the risk of giving man a measure of real freedom, he took the risk that man would abuse that freedom. Once God created the possibilities of man's self-awareness to match his freedom, he opened the way for human self-evaluation and self-criticism. Man therefore can know both self-respect and shame, pride and humility. He is part of nature, and yet above nature. He is an animal, yet more than an animal. In this lies his glory and his tragedy. His self-awareness permits him to watch himself in action. It makes it possible for him to imagine what he would like to be and then try to be it. It also means that he is inevitably tantalized by ideals which he can never completely forget. He cannot settle for being merely an animal, operating on impulse, never looking back or ahead or up. Nor can he achieve any sort of angelic state, divorced from his involvement in nature. Thus there is always something ambiguous about his image of himself: he sins and errs and makes mistakes and yet he cannot lightly forgive himself, nor can he utterly condemn himself. He always walks a tightrope; he runs the risk of falling off into either complacency or hopelessness.

He can decide to summon up all his energy to coerce reality to do his bidding. He can try to be master of his fate and captain of his soul, asserting his independence, and creating for himself the illusion of sovereignty over circumstance. Or he may settle for something a little less melodramatic, and, admitting that he is no superman, do the best he can with what he has without external help, in the mood of Sarah Teasdale's poem, "Mastery":

"I would not have a god come in
To shield me suddenly from sin,
And set my house of life to rights;
Nor angels with bright burning wings
Ordering my earthly thoughts and things;
Rather my own frail guttering lights
Windblown and nearly beaten out,
Rather the terror of the nights
And long sick groping after doubt.
Rather be lost than let my soul
Slip vaguely from my own control—
Of my own spirit let me be
In sole, though feeble, mastery."

Or he can, as Huxley advised, sit down before the facts as a little child and follow wherever they lead. His mood does not need to be belligerently existentialist; he can listen and think and learn and experiment; he can be humble, receptive and teachable. And if he is, his "situation" may suddenly become clearer: he was born into an amazing universe whose history stretches back into the infinite past and whose promise reaches forward into the infinite future; he had nothing to do with the selection of the century in which he appeared, the country, culture, tradition and family in which his life was nurtured. His capacities and powers were given to him, and, when traced back, depend ultimately on the mysterious life-processes which brought man up through the unconscious period of instinct to the self-conscious period of choice and responsibility. Well might Paul write to the Corinthians, "What hast thou that thou didst not *receive*?" [6]

We do not hear, as much as we used to, about "self-made" men. When Joseph Parker heard someone claim to be self-made, his reply was, "Well, sir, that relieves the Lord of a great responsibility." We shall never be able to know just how much of what we accomplish is the result of our own efforts. Some people seem to be moulded almost entirely by circumstances over which they exercise little control, and others seem to have reshaped what nature, family and opportunity give them from the time of childhood on, placing an unmistakable personal stamp on everything they do. But the more one ponders his own situation, the less he is apt to claim having been the chief determiner of his own destiny. Suppose he loves music: he is indebted to all those who slaved to create the magnificent musical tradition of our civilization. Suppose he is inspired by great painting: it is the same story. Suppose he becomes a composer or performer or painter. It is futile to wonder how much of his success is due to heredity, environment, education or sheer application on his part. He "received" both ability and opportunity.

But he also may have "received" serious limitations. He may be the victim of conditions he did not create which prevent him from being what he would like to become.

Life and literature are full of examples of "cry babies" and "sore-heads" who spend their time whimpering or complaining about the raw deal they received. But I taught a man in theological seminary who was born without arms, and the way he has carried on without them has been an inspiration to the handicapped during his whole life. The Helen Kellers of the world expend no energy in self-pity; they do what they can with what they were given.

There is no even-handed justice about what people receive. The image of an anthropomorphic God who, like a toy-manufacturer, puts out each creation with the exact characteristics he chooses, is not a helpful conception. But the image of a Super-Personal Power, who can be thought of in terms of the best we know, whose control of the farthest galaxies is beyond our capacity to imagine, but whose presence with us as we pray has the nature of loving concern that Jesus showed to those who knew him in the days of his flesh—this image can make all the difference between life and mere existence. If we accept him and believe in him, we then will be grateful for what we have received. We can be loyal to him in what we do with our gifts and talents. We will still stumble and sin, we will still suffer and doubt, but we will come to know what the Psalmist meant when he cried, "Underneath are the everlasting arms," and what Paul meant when he preached, "God that made the world and all things therein, seeing that he is Lord of heaven and earth, dwelleth not in temples made with hands; neither is worshipped with men's hands, as though he needed anything, seeing he giveth to all life, and breath, and all things; and hath made of one blood all nations of men for to dwell on the face of the earth, . . . that they should seek the Lord, if haply they might feel after him, and find him, though he be not far from every one of us: for in him we live, and move, and have our being."[7] In this conception, man's imagination has projected an image of Deity which is worthy of his mature faith, and which he believes is the product of God's self-revelation.

Notes

CHAPTER 1

1. John C. Bennett, *Christianity and Our World* (*Hazen Books on Religion,* New York: Association Press, 1936), p. 7
2. Quoted, among other *Russellisms,* in *The Saturday Review,* Jan. 25, 1958, p. 15
3. "The Anthropology of God" in the *Union Seminary Quarterly Review* (published by Union Theological Seminary, New York, November, 1957), p. 16
4. Lincoln Barnett, *The Universe and Dr. Einstein* (New York: William Sloane Associates, 1948), p. 105
5. Ibid., p. 106

CHAPTER 2

1. Joseph Wood Krutch, *The Modern Temper* (New York: Harcourt, Brace, 1929), p. 9
2. Bertrand Russell, *Selected Papers* (New York: Modern Library, 1927; London: Allen & Unwin), p. 3
3. Joseph Wood Krutch, *The Modern Temper* (New York: Harcourt, Brace, 1929), Preface, p. xvi
4. H. L. Mencken, *Prejudices, Third Series* (New York: Knopf, 1922), p. 132
5. Joseph Wood Krutch, *The Modern Temper* (New York: Harcourt, Brace, 1929), p. 249
6. Ibid., pp. 21–22
7. Bertrand Russell, *Selected Papers* (New York: Modern Library, 1927; London: Allen & Unwin), p. 158
8. *The Saturday Review,* September, 1957, p. 13
9. Matthew 5:45
10. Henry Nelson Wieman, *Religious Experience and Scientific Method* (New York, Macmillan, 1926), p. 9
11. Joseph Fort Newton, ed., *My Idea of God* (Boston: Little, Brown, 1926), pp. 237 ff.
12. Ibid., p. 191
13. Ibid., p. 189
14. Ralph Waldo Emerson, *Miscellanies* (Boston: Houghton Mifflin, 1868), p. 120
15. Walter Marshall Horton, *Theism and the Modern Mood* (New York: Harper, 1930), pp. 106 ff.
16. Paul Tillich, *Systematic Theology, Volume I* (Chi-

cago: University of Chicago Press, 1951), p. 235
17. Psalm 2:4
18. John 4:24
19. Psalm 137:5
20. Matthew 23:37
21. Harry Emerson Fosdick, *The Secret of Victorious Living* (New York: Harper, 1934), p. 152
22. Psalm 94:9
23. William Adams Brown, *God at Work* (New York, Scribners, 1932), p. 192

CHAPTER 3

1. John Baillie, *The Idea of Revelation in Recent Thought* (New York: Columbia University Press, 1956), p. 72
2. William Foxwell Albright, *From the Stone Age to Christianity* (New York: Doubleday, 1957), p. 249.
3. Ibid., p. 261
4. I assume that Genesis 1 is much later than Genesis 3
5. William Foxwell Albright, *From the Stone Age to Christianity* (New York: Doubleday, 1957), p. 265
6. II Kings 23:7; Hosea 4:13–14
7. Micah 6:8
8. Hosea 1:2
9. Isaiah 43:10
10. Isaiah 44:6
11. Nehemiah 6:3
12. Harry Emerson Fosdick, *A Guide to Understanding the Bible* (New York: Harper, 1938), p. 33.
13. Isaiah 19:24–25
14. Isaiah 49:23
15. Zechariah 14:9
16. Zechariah 14:17
17. Psalm 3
18. Isaiah 66:13
19. Psalm 103:13
20. Exodus 33:11
21. Hosea 2:20
22. Jeremiah 3:14
23. See Psalms 3, 5, 6, 12, 14, 15, 47 and 60 as examples
24. See Psalms 23, 46, 91, 100, 122 as examples
25. Luke 17:2; Matthew 18:6
26. Matthew 25:41, 46
27. Matthew 19:17
28. Hebrews 4:15
29. John 3:16
30. John 3:17
31. John 8:55
32. John 10:38
33. John 10:30
34. John 14:28
35. John 5:19, 30
36. John 5:36
37. John 7:16
38. II Corinthians 4:6
39. II Corinthians 4:4
40. John 14:9
41. I John 4:16

CHAPTER 4

1. Psalm 25:9
2. Psalm 32:8
3. Psalm 78:52
4. II Chronicles 32:22
5. Psalm 48:14
6. Isaiah 8:19
7. Proverbs 1:23
8. Matthew 4:8–10
9. Matthew 4:1–7
10. Matthew 12:28

11. Matthew 12:32, with parallels in Mark and Luke
12. Acts 10:19–20
13. Acts 8:26
14. Acts 16:7
15. Acts 19:21
16. Acts 20:23
17. The evidence is not completely conclusive: Luke 9:50 must be balanced off against Matthew 12:30, but Jesus undoubtedly believed the Father's cause to be his own
18. Galatians 5:22, 23
19. Arthur Cushman McGiffert, *A History of Christian Thought, Volume II* (New York: Scribners, 1932), p. 87

CHAPTER 5

1. Quoted by Hans Lilje in *The Student World,* Fourth Quarter, 1933, p. 325
2. H. E. Fosdick, *Great Voices of the Reformation* (New York: Modern Library 1952), p. 72
3. E. H. Harbison, *The Age of Reformation* (Ithaca: Cornell, 1955), p. 65
4. Ibid., p. 77
5. *Institutes,* III, 21, 7
6. John Calvin, *Instruction in Faith, 1537,* trans. P. T. Fuhrmann (Philadelphia: Westminster Press, 1949)
7. *Institutes,* III 23, 2
8. H. E. Fosdick, *Great Voices of the Reformation* (New York: Modern Library, 1952), p. 197
9. Ibid., p. 201
10. John Wesley, *Works, Volume I,* p. 194
11. Ibid., *Volume VIII,* p. 220
12. H. Martin P. Davidson, *Good Christian Men* (New York: Scribners, 1954), p. 218. The whole book is well worth reading.

CHAPTER 6

1. Victor C. Kitchen, *I Was a Pagan* (New York: Harper, 1934), p. 120
2. Ibid., p. 121

CHAPTER 7

1. Leo Rosten, editor, *A Guide to the Religions of America* (New York: Simon and Schuster, 1955), p. 93
2. Horton Davies, *Christian Deviations* (New York: Philosophical Library, 1954), p. 78
3. Revelation 7:4
4. Leo Rosten, editor, *A Guide to the Religions of America* (New York: Simon and Schuster, 1955), p. 133
5. Horton Davies, *Christian Deviations* (New York: Philosophical Library, 1954), p. 22
6. Ibid., p. 24
7. Ibid., p. 25
8. Mary Baker Eddy, *Science and Health,* p. 113
9. Ibid., p. 413
10. Leo Rosten, editor, *A Guide to the Religions of America*

(New York: Simon and Schuster, 1955), p. 22
11. *Science and Health,* p. 277

CHAPTER 8

1. William Graham Cole, *Sex in Christianity and Psychoanalysis* (New York: Oxford University Press, 1955), p. 286
2. I Samuel 15:22
3. *Time,* October 21, 1957, p. 64
4. W. Douglas Mackenzie, *The Ethics of Gambling* (New York: Doubleday, Doran, 1928), p. 25
5. *New York Herald Tribune,* August 19, 1957, Section 3, p. 1
6. S. Lorand, editor, *Psychoanalysis Today* (New York: Ronald Press, 1944), p. 32

CHAPTER 9

1. *Hymns for Colleges and Schools,* edited by E. Harold Geer (New Haven: Yale University Press, 1956; London: Oxford University Press)
2. Francis Henry Taylor, *Fifty Centuries of Art* (New York: Harper, 1954), p. 55
3. Bernard Rosenberg and David Manning White, editors, *Mass Culture, The Popular Arts in America* (New York: Free Press, 1957), p. 15
4. Available by writing to *Christianity and Arts Associated,* 297 Fourth Avenue, New York 10, N.Y.
5. Archibald Thompson Davison, *Church Music, Illusion and Reality* (Cambridge: Harvard University Press, 1952), Preface, p. ix
6. Ibid., p. 129
7. Ibid., p. 130
8. Archibald Thompson Davison, *Protestant Church Music in America* (Boston: E. C. Schirmer, 1933), p. 58
9. Ibid., p. 9

CHAPTER 10

1. Walter Marshall Horton, *A Psychological Approach to Theology* (New York: Harper, 1931), p. 223
2. Ibid., p. 196
3. John Baillie, *The Place of Jesus Christ in Modern Christianity* (New York: Scribners, 1929), p. 201
4. Quoted by Harry Emerson Fosdick in *The Meaning of Faith* (New York: Association Press, 1921), p. 145
5. *The Meaning of Faith,* Chapter VI
6. I Corinthians 4:7
7. Acts 17:24–28

Index

Index

This book deals with the images of God which have stimulated man's imagination. With the increase in concern and conversation about religion, the Deity is being characterized in many extraordinary ways. The idea which man has of God will naturally have a definite bearing on all his beliefs and an influence on his actions. To some he is "the Cosmic Mathematician," to others, "the Man Upstairs." Vital questions like the following are raised on all sides: Is God conscious, personal, super-personal? How does he guide us? What does he want us to do and be? Is he interested in our peace of mind? Does he get angry with us if we sin? What are his attributes?

Dr. Harris in a very original way examines the various images of God which have been handed on to us or which are currently being popularized. The structural plan of the contents follows these main headings:

IMAGES OF GOD
THE GOD OF THE THEIST
THE GOD OF THE BIBLE
THE GOD OF OUR TRADITION
THE GOD OF THE GODLY
THE GOD OF THE GUIDED
THE GOD OF CULTS AND SECTS
THE GOD OF THE RIGHTEOUS
THE GOD OF HYMN AND SONG
MAN'S IMAGE AND GOD'S